SEVEN REALITIES FOR

EXPERIENCING

GOD

How to Know and Do the Will of God

HENRY & RICHARD BLACKABY

LifeWay Press®
Nashville, Tennessee

Published by LifeWay Press® • © 2014 Henry Blackaby and Richard Blackaby • Reprinted 2018

No part of this book may be reproduced or transmitted in any form or by any means, electronic or mechanical, including photocopying and recording, or by any information storage or retrieval system, except as may be expressly permitted in writing by the publisher. Requests for permission should be addressed in writing to LifeWay Press®; One LifeWay Plaza; Nashville, TN 37234.

ISBN 978-1-4300-3655-5 • Item 005693757

Dewey decimal classification: 231 • Subject headings: SPIRITUAL LIFE \ CHRISTIAN LIFE \ GOD

To order additional copies of this resource, write to LifeWay Resources Customer Service; One LifeWay Plaza; Nashville, TN 37234; fax 615-251-5933; phone toll free 800-458-2772; email orderentry@lifeway.com; order online at LifeWay.com; or visit the LifeWay Christian Store serving you.

Printed in the United States of America

Groups Ministry Publishing • LifeWay Resources • One LifeWay Plaza • Nashville, TN 37234

CONTENTS

The Authors

Henry T. Blackaby is the founder and president emeritus of Blackaby Ministries International, an organization built to help people experience God.

Born in British Columbia, Henry has devoted his lifetime to ministry, serving churches in California and Canada. He was the president of Canadian Baptist Theological College for seven years and the president of the Canadian Southern Baptist Conference. He has provided leadership to thousands of pastors and laymen across North America and has spoken to missionaries and other groups in over 90 countries.

Henry went on to serve at the North American Mission Board of the Southern Baptist Convention and as a special assistant to the presidents of the International Mission Board and LifeWay Christian Resources. Although officially retired, he continues to provide consultative leadership in the Christian community.

Henry is a graduate of the University of British Columbia and earned his BD and ThM from Golden Gate Baptist Theological Seminary. He holds four honorary-doctorate degrees. He has published an array of spiritually influential messages in his lifetime, including *Experiencing God: Knowing and Doing the Will of God, Experiencing God Together,* and *Experiencing God Day by Day.*

Henry lives with his wife, Marilynn, in Rex, Georgia. They have five children, all of whom are serving in Christian ministry, and 14 grandchildren.

Richard Blackaby is the president of Blackaby Ministries International. He travels internationally, speaking on spiritual leadership in the home, church, and market-place; spiritual awakening; experiencing God; and the Christian life. He regularly ministers to Christian CEOs and business leaders.

Richard grew up in Saskatoon, Saskatchewan, Canada, and earned a BA from the University of Saskatchewan. He also has an MDiv and PhD from Southwestern Baptist Theological Seminary and an honorary doctorate from Dallas Baptist University.

Richard served as the senior pastor of Friendship Baptist Church in Winnipeg and then as the president of the Canadian Southern Baptist Seminary in Cochrane, Alberta, Canada, for 13 years. He continues to serve as the seminary's chancellor.

Richard has written or coauthored over 30 books, including *The Seasons of God, The Inspired Leader, Unlimiting God,* and *Putting a Face on Grace.* He also served as a managing editor and coauthor of the Blackaby Study Bible.

Richard and his wife of 29 years, Lisa, live in Atlanta, Georgia. They have three children.

About This Study

Within the heart of every Christian is the innate
desire to know God and to do His will.

God knows what your life can become. Only He understands your full potential as His child. He doesn't want you to miss out on anything He has for you.

Do you believe that? God wants you to know His will. He's not trying to hide it from you. But so often Christians genuinely wonder and even worry about how to know and do the will of God.

You may be immersed in Bible studies and books that provide an enormous amount of information about God. You may have sermon notes stuffed between the pages of your Bible. But do you live in the joy and satisfaction of fellowship with God?

To many people, He's simply a faraway God to be believed in, a doctrine to affirm, an invisible Deity to whom they recite prayers. We need to remember that God is a Person with whom Christians can enjoy an intimate, growing, loving relationship.

You may be frustrated as a Christian because you know God has a more abundant life for you than you're presently experiencing. Or you may earnestly desire God's directions for your life as you seek to serve Him. Perhaps you've recently experienced tragedy, and now you stand bewildered in the middle of a broken life, not knowing what to do next. Whatever your circumstances, my sincere prayer is that this study will help you do the following.

☐ Believe and experience daily God's infinite love for you.
☐ Hear when God is speaking to you.
☐ Identify God's unmistakable activity in your life.
☐ Believe God to be and do everything He promises.
☐ Adjust your beliefs, character, and behavior to God and His ways.
☐ Identify a direction God is taking in your life and recognize what He wants to do through you.
☐ Know clearly how to respond to what God shows you.
☐ Experience God doing through you what only He can do.

How to Use This Study

Seven Realities for Experiencing God is an eight-session Bible study. Most groups meet weekly, completing one session each week, but whenever your group decides to meet, it's important that participants commit to both parts of this Bible study: personal and group study.

The first group session is an introduction to the Seven Realities and the life of Moses, who will serve as the primary biblical example for experiencing God. Following this introductory group session, each week's study will focus on one of the Seven Realities, for a total of eight sessions.

Each reality provides content for **personal study**, including five short, daily readings with reflection questions to complete before gathering as a group. Optional journaling pages are also provided following the fifth day of study. These extra pages provide space to record any thoughts, questions, or experiences related to the week's study.

Each reality provides content for **group study,** structured in the following way.

START

This section includes prompts to start your group session with review and prayer.

READ & RESPOND

This section includes a passage of Scripture to read aloud and questions to lead a discussion of what the passage reveals about one of the Seven Realities.

REVIEW

This section includes questions for personal application of the Scripture studied, drawing from selected questions in the daily readings. This section ties together the personal and group content.

EXPERIENCING GOD STORIES

This section gives group members an opportunity to share stories about how they've experienced God in ways related to the reality they've studied.

WRAP UP

This section includes a statement that summarizes the group session, a statement giving instructions for and a preview of the next week's study, and a prompt to close in prayer.

Tips for Leading a Group

PRAYERFULLY PREPARE

Prepare for each session by—

☐ reviewing the weekly material and group questions ahead of time;

☐ praying for each person in the group.

Ask the Holy Spirit to work through you and the group discussion as you point to Jesus each week through God's Word.

MINIMIZE DISTRACTIONS

Create a comfortable environment. If group members are uncomfortable, they'll be distracted and therefore not engaged in the group experience. Plan ahead by taking into consideration—

☐ seating;

☐ temperature;

☐ lighting;

☐ food or drink;

☐ surrounding noise;

☐ general cleanliness (put pets away if meeting in a home).

At best, thoughtfulness and hospitality show guests and group members they're welcome and valued in whatever environment you choose to gather. At worst, people may never notice your effort, but they're also not distracted. Do everything in your ability to help people focus on what's most important: connecting with God, with the Bible, and with others.

INCLUDE OTHERS

Your goal is to foster a community in which people are welcome just as they are but encouraged to grow spiritually. Always be aware of opportunities to—

☐ invite new people to join your group;

☐ include any people who visit the group.

An inexpensive way to make first-time guests feel welcome or to invite people to get involved is to give them their own copies of this Bible-study book.

ENCOURAGE DISCUSSION

A good small group has the following characteristics.

- ☐ Everyone participates. Encourage everyone to ask questions, share responses, or read aloud.
- ☐ No one dominates—not even the leader. Be sure what you say takes up less than half of your time together as a group. Politely redirect discussion if anyone dominates.
- ☐ Nobody is rushed through questions. Don't feel that a moment of silence is a bad thing. People often need time to think about their responses to questions they've just heard or to gain courage to share what God is stirring in their hearts.
- ☐ Input is affirmed and followed up. Make sure you point out something true or helpful in a response. Don't just move on. Build personal connections with follow-up questions, asking how other people have experienced similar things or how a truth has shaped their understanding of God and the Scripture you're studying. People are less likely to speak up if they fear that you don't actually want to hear their answers or that you're looking for only a certain answer.
- ☐ God and His Word are central. Opinions and experiences can be helpful, but God has given us the truth. Trust Scripture to be the authority and God's Spirit to work in people's lives. You can't change anyone, but God can. Continually point people to the Word and to active steps of faith.

KEEP CONNECTING

Think of ways to connect with group members during the week. Participation during the group session is always improved when members spend time connecting with one another away from the session. The more people are comfortable with and involved in one another's lives, the more they'll look forward to being together. Encourage group members with thoughts, commitments, or questions from the session by connecting through emails, texts, and social media.

When possible, build deeper friendships by planning or spontaneously inviting group members to join you outside your regularly scheduled group time for meals; fun activities; and projects around your home, church, or community.

A GOD-CENTERED LIFE

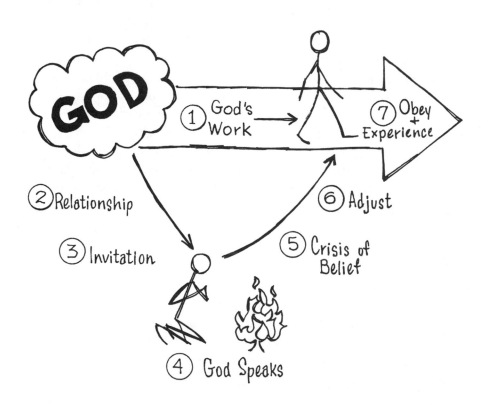

The Bible is God-centered. Never forget that every time you open the Scriptures, you're face-to-face with the Author. The Bible is more than just a Book. It's God's Word. In it the Creator of the universe is speaking to you. Do you believe that? It's true. But the Bible isn't about you. It's about God and how you can truly know Him.

The ancient Hebrew idea of knowing is one of experience; you can't really know something without experiencing it. So the only way to know God is to experience Him. The more you experience Him, the more you know Him. So every time you read His Word, He's making Himself known.

Fortunately, God has assigned the Holy Spirit to be your Teacher. You can't come to know God in your own wisdom. The Holy Spirit points you toward the Father and toward the Lord Jesus. He opens your mind and your heart to Him. When your life starts to become God-oriented, you see that God has an agenda you knew nothing about. He has a mission.

When you open the Scriptures, you begin to see what He's doing in you and all around you. The Bible is designed to help you understand the ways of God. Then, when God starts to use your life in the same way He worked in Scripture, you'll recognize that it's God who's at work in you and through you. Moses' experience at the burning bush clearly illustrates the way God invites ordinary people to experience Him in extraordinary ways. Throughout Scripture a common pattern surfaces that I call the Seven Realities for experiencing God. The Seven Realities identify ways God works to involve people in His activity.

1. God is always at work around you.
2. God pursues a continuing love relationship with you that is real and personal.
3. God invites you to become involved with Him in His work.
4. God speaks by the Holy Spirit through the Bible, prayer, circumstances, and the church to reveal Himself, His purposes, and His ways.
5. God's invitation for you to work with Him always leads you to a crisis of belief that requires faith and action.
6. You must make major adjustments in your life to join God in what He is doing.
7. You come to know God by experience as you obey Him, and He accomplishes His work through you.

These Seven Realities describe the ongoing experience of a God-centered life.

INTRODUCTORY GROUP SESSION
A GOD-CENTERED LIFE

START

If people don't already have their Bible-study books, start by distributing *Seven Realities for Experiencing God*.

Take a few minutes for group members to introduce themselves and to share their hopes for this eight-week study.

Always be sure to pray before beginning your time in God's Word. Ask God to make His will known and to change each person's life over the next eight weeks together.

READ & RESPOND

Read the following statement aloud.

> The Bible is designed to help you understand
> the ways of God. Then, when God starts to use
> your life in the same way He worked in Scripture,
> you'll recognize that it's God who's at work.

Use the following questions to discuss Hebrews 11 and a God-centered life. (Refer to p. 11 for an overview of a God-centered life, if needed.)

Read Hebrews 11:1-2.

How did the writer of Hebrews define *faith* in verse 1?

How would you explain that statement in your own words?

Read Hebrews 11:6.

According to verses 2 and 6, what's the relationship between faith and experiencing God?

Verses 2 and 6 mention God's approval or commendation, God's pleasure, and God's reward. How do faith and seeking nearness to God relate to these ideas?

How would you explain the difference between merely believing God exists and seeking to draw near to Him by faith?

Read Hebrews 11:23-29.

What common factor do these verses emphasize in the ways Moses experienced God?

Read the following statement aloud.

These verses include just some of the events in Moses' life and the exodus of God's people from slavery in Egypt. This summary doesn't even mention the miraculous encounters with God, provision in the wilderness, receiving the Ten Commandments, the plagues in Egypt, or the burning bush where the Lord called Moses to join His work.

What does Hebrews 11 teach us about a God-centered life?

Read the following statement aloud.

> The life of Moses is one of many that could be used
> to demonstrate how believers can experience God.
> We'll look closely at Moses' life each week as a
> model of the Seven Realities for experiencing God.

REFLECT

In the following sessions the group will review Bible-study material that group members read during the week and will relate it to your group study. For this introductory session, further reflect on what you've read in Hebrews.

How does your life demonstrate faith in God?

By what ways other than faith have you tried to earn God's approval?

How have those pursuits affected your relationship with God?

Hebrews 11:6 says, "Without faith it is impossible to please God." What's your response to that verse?

One way to better understand Scripture is to reword negative statements as positive or positive statements as negative. How would you restate the truth of Hebrews 11:6 in positive terms?

One of the most common questions asked by people who are seeking to please God and live by faith is "How do I know and do the will of God?" When have you wanted to know God's will? What did you do?

How are you currently seeking to draw near to God and know His will?

EXPERIENCING GOD STORIES

Each week you'll have an opportunity to share how you've experienced God.

Would anyone like to share a story of how you've experienced God as He rewarded your faith or as He drew near when you sought Him?

How have you experienced confidence and assurance of faith, as described in Hebrews 11:1?

WRAP UP

Conclude the session by reading this final thought and then closing in prayer.

"What is God's will for my life?" isn't the best question to ask. "What is God's will, and how can I join Him in that?" is the better question. Too often we want to plan our own lives and call God in to make us successful. But when we're living God-centered lives, we understand that God has better plans that He invites us to join.

Remind members to read the daily devotions for Reality 1 before your next group session. In addition to the devotional readings and journaling pages that follow day 5, people may want to read Exodus 1–20 to have the full story of Moses fresh in mind before closely examining the Seven Realities for experiencing God.

Next week we'll discuss Reality 1:
God is always at work around you.

REALITY 1
GOD'S WORK

God is always at work around you.

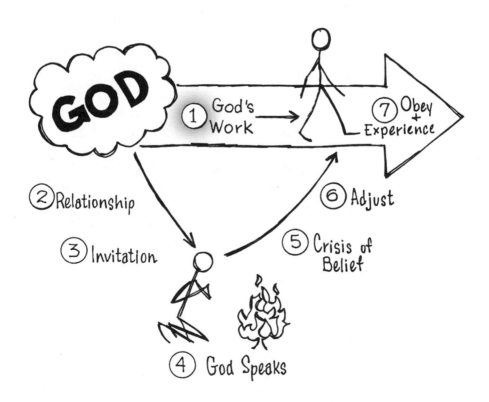

God didn't create the world and then abandon it to function on its own. He's been actively involved in human affairs throughout history. In fact, He's orchestrating history. Because of sin, humanity has been separated from a close relationship with God. God is working in His world to bring about the redemption of those who are alienated from Him and facing imminent judgment and destruction. The Father is working through Christ to reconcile the world to Himself. In God's sovereignty He's chosen to accomplish His work through His people. As He carries out His mission, He seeks to move people into the mainstream of His activity.

God was already at work around Moses' life when He encountered Moses at the burning bush. God had a purpose He was steadily working out in Moses' world. Even though Moses was an exile in the desert, he was right on God's schedule, in the fullness of God's timing, in the middle of God's will for that moment.

Years earlier God told Abraham that his descendants would be in bondage but that He would deliver them and give them the promised land. God was watching and waiting for the right time to carry out His purpose for Israel.

At the time God was about to deliver the children of Israel, the overriding concern was His will for Israel, not His will for Moses. God was at work with Israel, and He was preparing to bring Moses into the mainstream of His activity to redeem His people.

This truth also applies to your life. God is actively working in the lives of people around you, even when you don't recognize it. However, unless God opens your spiritual eyes to recognize what He's doing, you'll remain blind to His presence and His work.

day 1
MIRACULOUS ACTIVITY

*Now get up and stand on your feet. I have appeared
to you to appoint you as a servant and as a witness
of what you have seen and will see of me.*
ACTS 26:16

God was working in your life long before you began following Him. The Lord knew you before time began, and He knew what He wanted to do with your life (see Ps. 139:13; Jer. 1:5).

Before the apostle Paul's conversion experience on the road to Damascus, Jesus already knew Paul and had a specific assignment for him. But Jesus revealed this assignment only after Paul's conversion (see Acts 9:15). Paul was so misguided that in his sincere efforts to serve God, he had actually been waging war against Christians. Although God knew what He wanted for Paul, He waited to reveal it to him until He gained his attention and became his Lord.

Our Lord doesn't come to us to discover what we'd like to accomplish for Him. He encounters us in order to reveal His activity and invite us to become involved in His work. An encounter with God requires us to adjust ourselves to the activity of God that's been revealed. God never communicates with us merely to give us a warm devotional thought for the day. He never speaks to us simply to increase our biblical knowledge. Our Lord has far more significant things to reveal to us than that. When God shows us what He's doing, He invites us to join Him in His activity.

Do you want to experience God today? Don't seek to hear from God unless you're ready to ask, as Paul did, "What shall I do, Lord?" (Acts 22:10).

As you read the accounts of God's miraculous work through men and women in the Bible, you may wonder whether God still performs such miracles today. Be assured that the same God who walked with Moses, Joshua, Elijah, Peter, James, John, and Paul now lives within you. No power can defeat the God who guides you. The God who blessed them is just as capable of working out His purposes through your life. The same God who gave them victory over seemingly invincible enemies, who provided for them when their own resources were insufficient, and who guided them in their decisions is prepared to work as powerfully in your life today.

Too often we acknowledge our belief that God can do whatever He wants; then we add a safety clause: "But I just don't think God will do that with me." We become practical atheists, believing God can perform miracles but never expecting a miracle in our own lives.

The heroes of the faith had one thing in common: they were all ordinary people with no power of their own. The difference was the mighty presence of God. Times may change, but the miraculous effect of God's presence remains the same.

When did you first experience God?[1] Whom did He work through to bring you to faith through the gospel? Record as many details as you can remember about your conversion story. Consider what your life would be like if God hadn't been at work to save you. How is your story a miracle?

In what specific area of your life do you struggle to believe that God is at work and has a plan?

What was the most meaningful statement or Scripture you read today?

Reword the statement or Scripture into a prayer of response to God.

What does God want you to do in response to today's study?

---

1. If you haven't experienced God by first responding in faith to the work of Jesus Christ, go to the back of this book to learn how to begin a personal relationship with God.

day 2

THE ONGOING WORK OF SALVATION

*Work out your salvation with fear and trembling,
for it is God who works in you to will and to
act in order to fulfill his good purpose.*
PHILIPPIANS 2:12-13

Salvation isn't just an event; it's also a process. Salvation is God's gift, for there's nothing we can do to save ourselves (see Eph. 2:8-9). Yet with salvation comes the responsibility to work out our salvation.

This is the great paradox of the Christian life. We're to work diligently on our faith yet always with the awareness that only God can bring about lasting change in our lives. As we see God at work in us, we're motivated to work even more diligently.

God won't force His changes on us; neither can we bring about lasting change in our lives apart from the work of the Holy Spirit. An examination of the fruit of the Spirit can be intimidating (see Gal. 5:22-23). Working all nine of these traits into your life seems impossible, and indeed it is. But the moment you became a Christian, the Holy Spirit began a divine work to produce Christ's character in you. And He's always faithful to complete the work He begins (see Phil. 1:6).

Regardless of who you are, the Spirit works from the same model, Jesus Christ. The Spirit looks to Christ to supply the blueprint for your character. The Spirit immediately begins helping you experience and practice the same love Jesus had when He laid down His life for you, His friend (see John 15:13). The same joy He experienced will now fill you. The identical peace that guarded the heart of Jesus, even as He was being beaten and mocked, will be the peace the Spirit works to instill in you. The patience Jesus had for His seemingly unteachable disciples will be the patience the Spirit now develops in you. The kindness Jesus showed toward children and sinners will soften your heart toward others. There will be a goodness about you that can be explained only by the presence of the Spirit of God. The Spirit will build the same faith in you that led Jesus to be entirely obedient to His Father. The Spirit will teach you self-control so that you'll have strength to do what's right and to resist temptation. Because the Spirit lives in you, all this will occur as naturally as the growth of fruit on a tree.

You can't orchestrate spiritual growth on your own. It automatically begins the moment you become a believer. How quickly it happens depends on how completely you yield yourself to the Holy Spirit's activity. When you sense God developing an area of your life, join Him in His activity so that His salvation will be fully demonstrated in you.

What does God want to do in you? Have you allowed Him to complete what He has begun? He won't force you to receive all He has for your life. If God's work hasn't been brought to fruition in you, it's not that Christ hasn't been diligently working toward that end. Rather, you may need to release areas of your life to Him and be as determined as Christ is to see God's work completed in you.

How have you experienced the ongoing work of salvation as you've grown spiritually?

Where is the Spirit most evident in your life, producing the fruit described in Galatians 5:22-23?

What areas do you most struggle with in working out your salvation?

What was the most meaningful statement or Scripture you read today?

Reword the statement or Scripture into a prayer of response to God.

What does God want you to do in response to today's study?

day 3
A GOD-CENTERED PERSPECTIVE

The Spirit told Philip, "Go to that chariot and stay near it."
ACTS 8:29

God is always at work. He's on mission. What we call missions is simply God finding people whose hearts are spiritually prepared and placing them where they can make a difference for His kingdom. Some of the great missionaries in history didn't live long lives, but their lives dramatically affected eternity.

For example, God had Philip's attention, and the Book of Acts gives the exciting account of how He used Philip's life to take the gospel to the ends of the earth. Philip was powerfully preaching in the city of Samaria (see Acts 8:5-8). God used him so mightily that the entire city rejoiced at the miracles God was doing. This would be any evangelist's fondest desire: to see an entire city responding to the gospel through his preaching. Yet Philip wasn't activity-centered in his Christian life. He was God-centered. Philip wasn't preoccupied with expanding his reputation as a great preacher or miracle worker. He was concerned that his life remain in the center of God's activity.

When God instructed Philip to leave his fruitful ministry in Samaria, he didn't hesitate (see vv. 26-40). He was prepared. He was attentive. He experienced God by joining the mainstream of God's activity.

God continues to seek those as responsive as Philip to go on mission with Him. The reason God's movement isn't evident in more places today isn't that He's unable or unwilling to work. He first looks for those willing to have their lives radically adjusted away from their self-centered activities and placed in the center of God's activity around the world.

A God-centered perspective is the key to being spiritually prepared for God's work. If you're spiritually prepared when a crisis comes, you won't have to try to instantly develop the quality of relationship with Christ that can sustain you. If you have a God-centered focus and suddenly have an opportunity to share your faith with an unbeliever, you'll be equipped to do so. If you enter a time of worship spiritually prepared, you won't miss an encounter with God. If you're spiritually filled when you meet a person in sorrow, you'll have much to offer.

If you've established safeguards in your life in advance, you won't give in to temptation.

Christians lose many opportunities to experience God's activity because they haven't devoted enough time to their relationship with God. If you haven't yet developed the habit of daily prayer and Bible study, why not begin now so that you'll be spiritually equipped for whatever life brings?

How are you developing a God-centered perspective, spiritually preparing yourself to join God's work? Identify a time and a place in your daily routine that you can spend in prayer and Bible reading.

Identify an area of your life that's going well. What does it mean to have a God-centered perspective in that area of your life?

Identify an area of your life that's currently difficult. What does it mean to have a God-centered perspective in that area of your life?

What was the most meaningful statement or Scripture you read today?

Reword the statement or Scripture into a prayer of response to God.

What does God want you to do in response to today's study?

day 4
GOOD WORK OR GOD'S WORK

A Samaritan, as he traveled, came where the man
was; and when he saw him, he took pity on him.
LUKE 10:33

If anyone could understand the temptation to let busyness distract Him from the Father's activity, Jesus certainly could.

In Luke 10 He told a parable that clearly illustrated this danger. A certain Jewish man was on his way to Jericho when he was brutally attacked by thieves and left to die by the road. First a Levite, then a priest passed by. These were religious leaders; surely they'd show compassion to a wounded person. But they had places to go and appointments to keep, so they passed him by.

Then a Samaritan, despised by the Jews, came along. Of all people, this man had reason to look the other way since the wounded man was his enemy. But wherever he was going could wait, for someone needed his help.

It's easy to become so busy that you're oblivious to people in need. Your schedule can become so full of accomplishing good things that you're no help to the people around you.

God is at work in the lives of your friends, your neighbors, and your family members. He may ask you to interrupt your day long enough to join Him as He ministers to them. Nothing on your agenda, no matter how pressing, is reason enough to ignore the voice of God when He tells you to stop and help. If you've become too busy to minister to those around you, ask God to reestablish your priorities so that you don't miss opportunities to serve Him.

Even Jesus realized that His role was that of a servant (see Matt. 20:28). He never sought to initiate activity for the Father. A servant never sets the agenda; the master does. The servant must be so alert to what the master is doing that whenever the master begins to move in a direction, the servant quickly joins him. Jesus knew His Father so well that He was keenly sensitive to divine activity around Him, immediately recognizing His Father at work.

It's possible for us to be so busy trying to bring God into our activity that we don't notice Him at work around us. God seeks to redirect our attention so that we can join Him, but we tend to be self-centered, evaluating everything by the way it affects us. We must learn to view events around us from God's perspective. Then we'lll see our world very differently. When God brings someone across our path, we'll look to see whether God is convicting that person of the need for salvation. Perhaps God is comforting someone in sorrow. God might be encouraging one of your friends as he or she faces a challenge. We should then adjust our lives to join God as He works in that person's life. We ought to live each day with tremendous anticipation as we look to see where God is working around us. As our eyes are opened to His activity, we'll marvel at His great works.

On a scale of 1 to 10 (1 = overwhelmingly full schedule; 10 = wide open), how much room do you have in your daily routine?

On a scale of 1 to 10 (1 = definitely wouldn't; 10 = definitely would), how likely would you be to notice if God wanted to interrupt your plans?

On a scale of 1 to 10 (1 = definitely wouldn't; 10 = definitely would), how likely would you be to change your plans if God made you aware of an opportunity to join His work?

Honestly, which best describes your life in relation to God's will?
□ I never think about God's will.
□ I try to live a good life and hope God's pleased with it.
□ I make plans and ask for God's help to accomplish my daily activities.
□ I seek to know God's will and then change my life to join the work He's doing.

What was the most meaningful statement or Scripture you read today?

Reword the statement or Scripture into a prayer of response to God.

What does God want you to do in response to today's study?

PLACE AND PURPOSE

Now I want you to know, brothers and sisters, that what has happened to me has actually served to advance the gospel.
PHILIPPIANS 1:12

There are two ways to look at every situation: how it will affect you and how it will affect God's kingdom. The apostle Paul was always concerned with how his circumstances could aid the spread of the gospel. When he was unjustly imprisoned, he immediately looked to see how his imprisonment could bring God's salvation to others (see Acts 16:19-34; Phil. 1:13). When he was assailed by an angry mob, he used the opportunity to preach the gospel (see Acts 22:1-21). When Paul's criminal proceedings took him before King Agrippa, his thoughts were on sharing his faith with the king (see Acts 26). Even when Paul was shipwrecked on an island, he used that circumstance to join God's activity (see Acts 28:7-9). Regardless of his circumstance, Paul's concern was using his current situation to tell others of God's good news of salvation.

Often when we encounter a new situation, our first thoughts aren't about God's kingdom. When we face a crisis, we can become angry or fearful for our own well-being rather than looking to see what God intends to do through our circumstances. If we remain self-centered, we miss much of what God could do through our experiences, both for us and for those around us.

Will you dare to believe that God, who called you to Himself and equipped you with His Spirit, could work mightily through you? Have you made the connection between the time and place in which you live and God's call on you? He placed you precisely where you are for a purpose.

World events never catch God by surprise. History is replete with examples of Christian men and women who believed God would work through them to make a significant difference for His kingdom. God strategically placed Joseph to become the most powerful adviser to the pharaoh in Egypt and to save Jacob and his family from a devastating drought (see Gen. 41:39-40; 45:5-7). God strategically placed Esther in the king's court at a crucial time when she could save the lives of God's people (see Esth. 4:14).

The same God who was at work in and through the lives of biblical heroes is still at work today. Reading those stories, we may forget that real men and women had to trust God to work in incredibly difficult situations. We know the end of the story. But they were living in the middle of it.

You're a part of the same adventure—the narrative of God's kingdom. Wherever you are, the story's about Him. It's not about you. And because it's God's story, you can be sure He has a plan for where you are right now. He's doing something in you or through you for His purposes. God is always at work around you. Even if you don't understand, trust the One who says:

As the heavens are higher than the earth,
so are my ways higher than your ways
and my thoughts than your thoughts.
ISAIAH 55:9

There are two ways to look at every situation: how it will affect you and how it will affect God's kingdom. Which best describes your perspective?

How are you allowing your current situation to determine the way you invest your life?

How are you letting God use you to make a difference in your generation?

What was the most meaningful statement or Scripture you read today?

Reword the statement or Scripture into a prayer of response to God.

What does God want you to do in response to today's study?

How Am I Experiencing God?

Use this space to journal about your experience with God,
in particular Reality 1: God is always at work around you.

GROUP SESSION—REALITY 1
GOD IS ALWAYS AT WORK AROUND YOU

START

Start with review and prayer. Ask volunteers to summarize the truths discussed last week in the study of Hebrews 11:1-6,23-29.

Ask God to open your hearts and minds to the work He wants to do in and through your lives.

READ & RESPOND

Transition to a study of the biblical text and Reality 1. Read aloud Exodus 1–2.

Knowing that God would use Moses to confront Pharaoh and lead the Israelites out of slavery, discuss examples of Reality 1 in Exodus 1–2. (Refer to p. 17 for an overview of Reality 1, if needed.)

How was God at work during the birth of Moses (see 1:15–2:2)?

How was God at work during the childhood of Moses (see 2:1-10)?

How was God at work when Moses was a young man (see 2:15-25)?

In what way was God's work much bigger than just saving Moses' life (see 2:23-25)?

When we can't see God at work, what comfort comes from 2:24-25?

REVIEW

Continue the discussion on a personal level by connecting themes from the daily reading with Reality 1. (Allow these questions to serve as a guide, but feel free to discuss any meaningful statements from or actions taken in response to the daily reading.)

Day 1

In what specific area of your life do you struggle to believe that God is at work and has a plan?

What encouragement (and/or conviction) do you receive in knowing that the same God is at work in your life as in the lives of biblical heroes like Moses?

Day 2

In John 5:17 Jesus said, "My Father is always at his work to this very day, and I too am working." In what ways is God at work to shape your character for His purposes?

Day 3

What routines have you established in your life to keep you alert to God's work around you?

Day 4

In Exodus 2:11-15 Moses took matters into his own hands instead of looking to see how God was at work. When have you made a mess doing things through your own efforts or focusing too much on your own desires, thereby missing an opportunity to join God's work?

When have you experienced God by recognizing an opportunity to join His work?

Honestly, which of the following best describes your life in relation to God's will?

☐ I never think about God's will.
☐ I try to live a good life and hope God's pleased with it.
☐ I make plans and ask for God's help to accomplish my daily activities.
☐ I seek to know God's will and then change my life to join the work He's doing.

Day 5

God wasn't focused only on Moses' life. He was at work in and through Moses for the sake of a much bigger plan. You're not where you are in life by mistake or coincidence. How has God worked in your life through people or events you would otherwise consider to have been coincidental?

There are two ways to look at every situation: how it will affect you and how it will affect God's kingdom. Which best describes your perspective?

How could God use your present circumstances to bless others and make a difference in this generation?

How have you been challenged this week in regard to knowing and doing the will of God?

EXPERIENCING GOD STORIES

Use this opportunity to share ways you've experienced God.

Would anyone like to share a story about a time when you've experienced God's work in your life?

When have you felt that God might not care or know about your situation? Looking back, how did you experience God and see that He was always at work around you?

How might God's work in your life be for more than just your benefit?

WRAP UP

Conclude the session by reading this final thought and then closing in prayer.

The first reality for experiencing God is that God is always at work around you. God's work may go unnoticed at first, but His purpose is to move people into the mainstream of His activity. He's on mission to save people by His grace. Ultimately, this mission is even bigger than Moses and the Israelites in Egypt. God's mission is to save people through Jesus Christ. His Spirit is still at work in our lives today so that we too can know and do His will.

Next week we'll discuss Reality 2: God pursues a continuing love relationship with you that is real and personal.

RELATIONSHIP

God pursues a continuing love relationship
with you that is real and personal.

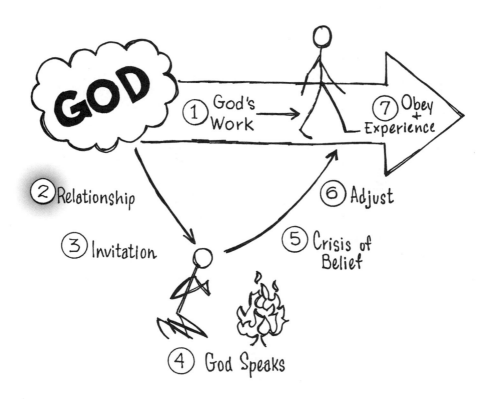

Real Christianity isn't merely a religion; it's a relationship with a Person. God created humanity for a love relationship with Him. More than anything else, God wants us to love Him with our total being (see Mark 12:30). He's the One who pursues a love relationship with us. We don't naturally seek God on our own initiative. Everything we're experiencing from God comes in response to His invitation. In fact, He dramatically reached out to us by sending His Son, Jesus (see John 3:16). God clearly demonstrated how valuable a love relationship is to Him when He permitted Jesus to die an excruciating death on a cross in order to make a relationship with us possible (see Rom. 5:8).

This intimate love relationship with God is both extremely personal and practical. This is probably the most important factor in knowing and doing the will of God. If your love relationship with God isn't as it should be, nothing else will be in order.

God took the lead in inviting Moses into a personal, dynamic relationship with Him. Moses had led the sheep he was tending to Horeb, the mountain of God. He was in the middle of his day, but God interrupted Moses' plans by encountering him at the burning bush.

Time and time again, God invited Moses to talk with Him and to be with Him. God initiated and maintained a growing relationship with Moses. The fellowship was based on love, and God daily fulfilled His purposes through Moses. This relationship with God was extremely practical as God guided and provided for His people under Moses' leadership.

day 1

MORE THAN RELIGIOUS KNOWLEDGE

You study the Scriptures diligently because you think that in them you have eternal life. These are the very Scriptures that testify about me, yet you refuse to come to me to have life.

JOHN 5:39-40

Bible study won't give you eternal life. You could memorize the entire Bible and be able to discuss minute issues of biblical scholarship and yet fail to experience the truths found in its pages. It's a subtle temptation to prefer the book to the Author, but a book won't confront you about your sin; the Author will. Books can be ignored; it's much harder to avoid the Author when He's seeking a relationship with you.

The Pharisees in Jesus' day thought God would be pleased with their knowledge of His Word. They could quote long, complicated passages of Scripture. They loved to recite and study God's law for hours on end. Yet Jesus condemned them because although they knew the Scriptures, they didn't know God. They were proud of their Bible knowledge, but they rejected the invitation to know God's Son.

Can you imagine knowing all God has promised to do in your life but then turning to something else instead? You may be tempted to turn to substitutes for a relationship with God. These substitutes aren't necessarily bad things in themselves. They might include serving in the church, doing good deeds, or reading Christian books.

Yet no amount of Christian activity will ever replace your relationship with Jesus. The apostle Paul considered everything he had ever done to be "garbage" when compared to the surpassing value of knowing Christ (Phil. 3:8). Never become satisfied with religious activity rather than a personal, vibrant, growing relationship with Jesus Christ.

Have you been reading the words of Jesus in your Bible without experiencing His word that transforms everything around you? Jesus condemned the Pharisees because they assumed that knowledge of the written Scriptures would give them life. They were satisfied with having the words instead of experiencing the person who spoke the words.

As you study your Bible, you may sense that God has something to say directly to you through the verses you're reading. Take a moment to consider the awesome reality that the God who spoke and created the universe is now speaking to you. If Jesus could speak and raise the dead, calm a storm, cast out demons, and heal the incurable, then what effect might a word from Him have on your life? The next time you open God's Word, do so with a sense of holy expectation.

On a scale of 1 to 10 (1 = dead or nonexistent; 10 = vibrant and growing), how would you describe your relationship with God?

What religious activity tends to become a focus of your spiritual life rather than strengthen your relationship with God? Why do you find yourself distracted by that particular discipline or activity?

What reminders can you use to approach religious (and seemingly ordinary) activities with a sense of holy expectation in order to experience God and strengthen your relationship with Him?

What was the most meaningful statement or Scripture you read today?

Reword the statement or Scripture into a prayer of response to God.

What does God want you to do in response to today's study?

day 2
THE JOY OF CHRIST

I am coming to you now, but I say these things
while I am still in the world, so that they may
have the full measure of my joy within them.
JOHN 17:13

If anything ought to characterize the life of a Christian, it's joy. Jesus spoke many times to His disciples about His joy being complete and full in them. His disciples were filled with joy as they realized who they were: children of God and joint heirs with Christ (see Rom. 8:16-17). They had been dead in their sins but were now made alive in Christ (see Rom. 6:4). They had once been helpless victims of death, but now death had no hold over them (see 1 Cor. 15:55-57). With such a marvelous salvation experience with Christ, how could the disciples be anything less than joyful?

It's not surprising that of all those who followed Jesus, Mary was the one to anoint His feet. The disciples would have opportunities to show the same love, but pride would prevent them (see John 13:1-17).

Martha too was prone toward acts of service, but she had developed a different kind of relationship with Jesus than Mary had. While Martha had labored on Jesus' behalf in the kitchen, Mary had joyfully sat at Jesus' feet and listened to Him teach (see Luke 10:38-42). Because Mary had come to know and love Jesus in this way, she was ready to humble herself and offer this poignant expression of love to Him. Such depth and sincerity of love come only by spending time in close fellowship with Jesus.

The way we express our love for Jesus depends on the kind of relationship we've developed with Him. Our love for Him won't grow unless we spend time with Him, listen to His voice, and experience His love for us. If we find that our love for Jesus has waned or that we struggle to serve Him, it's a clear sign that we must take time to sit at His feet. We may have been involved in Christian activity on His behalf and yet neglected our relationship with Him. After we've spent time in intimate fellowship with our Lord, heard His voice, and received His love, we'll be prepared to serve Him, even laying down our life for Him if that's what He asks.

Don't deny yourself your birthright as a child of God. Don't be satisfied with a joyless life. There ought to be in every Christian a deep, settled fullness of the joy of Christ that no circumstance of life can dispel. This kind of joy comes as you allow the Holy Spirit to express Himself in your life. One fruit of the Spirit is joy (see Gal. 5:22). This joy is unlike any happiness produced by the world. It fills you and permeates everything you do.

Jesus didn't pray that you'd merely be happy or even that you'd escape grief. He prayed that you'd have the same joy the Father had given Him: a divine joy that comes from a deep, unwavering relationship with the Father.

This joy is grounded so firmly in a relationship with God that no change in circumstances could ever shake it. This is the kind of joy that Christ is praying will be in you.

Before reading today's devotion, what word would you have used to describe the Christian life? Why?

Describe a time when you were filled with the joy of Christ.

How will you intentionally spend time developing your relationship with God?

What was the most meaningful statement or Scripture you read today?

Reword the statement or Scripture into a prayer of response to God.

What does God want you to do in response to today's study?

day 3
YOUR HEAVENLY FATHER

This is why I told you that no one can come
to me unless the Father has enabled them.
JOHN 6:65

Jesus often referred to God as Father. The word *father* conjures up different images for everyone. To some it brings a picture of love, laughter, respect, and acceptance. Unfortunately, others associate the term *father* with fear, rejection, and disappointment. These variations reveal why it's so important not to take your understanding of your Heavenly Father from your experience. Take it from Scripture. You undoubtedly had an imperfect earthly father, perhaps even one who harmed you. However, as in every dimension of your Christian life, the goal isn't to understand the Bible based on your experience but to understand your experience in light of the Bible. God is your model of a father in the truest sense of the word.

Your Heavenly Father was willing to pay any price in order to save you (see Rom. 8:32). Your Heavenly Father is always ready to meet your needs (see Luke 11:11-13). Your Heavenly Father loves you so much that He's willing to discipline you to bring you to Christian maturity (see Prov. 3:11-12; Heb. 12:5-10). Even when you rebel against Him and reject His love, your Father continues to do what's best for you (see Rom. 5:8). He doesn't make His love for you conditioned on your love for Him. He loves you even when you aren't loving Him (see 1 John 4:19). He has made you His heir and reserves a home for you in heaven (see John 14:2-3; Rom. 8:15-17).

These truths give a biblical picture of what a father is like. If this hasn't been your experience, it can be now. There's One who has adopted you and who wants to love you in a way you've never experienced.

Throughout Jesus' ministry on earth, He looked into the multitudes and focused on those whom His Father was sending to Him. Jesus knew that because of sin, no one naturally seeks God. Sinful man's inclination is to hide from God rather than to come to Him (see Gen. 3:8; Ps. 14:1-3). Therefore, whenever Jesus saw that the Father was drawing a person to Himself, Jesus immediately began relating to that person.

Jesus observed the great lengths to which the despised tax collector Zacchaeus had gone in order to see Him pass by. In response, Jesus immediately left the crowd and spent time with this man in whom the Father was obviously working (see Luke 19:1-10). Likewise, every time the disciples experienced a new insight into the truths of God, Jesus recognized that it was the Father who had been at work in their lives (see Matt. 16:17).

As the multitudes gathered around Jesus, He spoke some truths that were difficult for the people to grasp (see John 6:60). So challenging were His words that many of His listeners departed, but Jesus didn't become discouraged. He saw that the Father was working in the lives of His disciples, and that's where Jesus invested His time. When you want to spend time alone with Jesus, recognize that this desire is the Father drawing you to His Son. You don't seek quiet times with God in order to experience Him but because you already sense His activity in your heart and life. As you read the Scriptures and pray, trust that God will honor your response to His leading by teaching you more about Himself.

How does the word *father* help you better understand the character of God and what it means to be in a relationship with Him?

How have you experienced the Heavenly Father drawing your heart toward Jesus?

What was the most meaningful statement or Scripture you read today?

Reword the statement or Scripture into a prayer of response to God.

What does God want you to do in response to today's study?

day 4
GOD'S RELENTLESS LOVE

We know and rely on the love God has for us. God is love.
Whoever lives in love lives in God, and God in them.
1 JOHN 4:16

The greatest truth in all Scripture is this: God is love. Understanding this truth in its full dimensions will set you free to enjoy all that's yours as a Christian. But you must accept that God loves you. If you grew up experiencing unconditional love in your family, this may not be difficult for you. However, if your early years were void of love, this truth may be hard to accept. God loves you, not because you deserve His love but because His nature is love. The only way He will ever relate to you is in love. His love for you gives you an inherent worth that nothing can diminish.

No human can comprehend God's love for His children. Our limited experience of human love hinders us from understanding God's unconditional love for us. We can see a picture of this love in the life of Hosea.

Hosea was a righteous man, but God told him to marry a sinful woman. Hosea obeyed and took Gomer as his wife. He cherished her and treated her with dignity and respect. Never before had Gomer experienced this kind of love, but she soon grew dissatisfied. She began giving her affections to other men.

Gomer became so involved in adulterous pursuits that she finally abandoned Hosea altogether. Other men used her until she had nothing left to give. Then they sold her into slavery. After this, God gave Hosea an amazing command: "Go and buy her back" (author's paraphrase; see Hos. 3:1-2). Despite the intense pain and hurt that Gomer had inflicted on Hosea, God told him to forgive her and to pay any price to bring her back home.

God's message is clear: when we reject Him and turn our devotion elsewhere, our rejection carries the same pain as an adulterous betrayal. After all God has done for us, it's incomprehensible that we should reject Him. It's even harder to fathom that God could love us even after we've rejected, ignored, and disobeyed Him. Yet God's love is completely different from ours. His love follows us to the depths of our sinfulness until He's reclaimed us. His love is undaunted when we run from Him, and He continues to pursue us. What incredible love He's demonstrated to us!

If you can't accept the truth that God loves you, you'll be limited in the way you can relate to Him. When He disciplines you, you won't take it as an expression of His love. Rather, you may resent Him. When God says no to a request that's less than His best for you, you'll conclude that He doesn't care about you. Without a clear understanding and acceptance of God's love for you, you'll be disoriented to Him and to what He wants to do in your life. If you accept God's love, however, you'll be able to return love to God as well as to others (see 1 John 4:19).

Are you experiencing the profound sense of joy and security that comes from knowing that God dearly loves you? Being assured of God's love for you sets you free to enjoy the numerous expressions of love He showers on you each day.

When do you have the hardest time accepting the fact that God loves you? Why is it hard to feel loved by God? When is it easiest to believe that He loves you?

Describe a season in your life that resembles the unfaithful, ungrateful wandering of Gomer.

How does Hosea's example of God's relentless, loving pursuit of you change your view of God? Of yourself? Of a relationship with Him?

What was the most meaningful statement or Scripture you read today?

Reword the statement or Scripture into a prayer of response to God.

What does God want you to do in response to today's study?

day 5
UNIQUELY PERSONAL

When Jesus reached the spot, he looked up and
said to him, "Zacchaeus, come down immediately.
I must stay at your house today."
LUKE 19:5

In our large world it's easy to feel we're nothing more than an insignificant speck in the midst of a multitude. We may wonder whether God notices us or whether we can really know Him. Our world tends to depersonalize us, seeking to make us like everyone else, but God loves us in specific ways that are particular to us.

Jesus was on His way to Jerusalem to fulfill His assignment on the cross. The multitudes thronged around Him in such numbers that the diminutive Zacchaeus couldn't see Him unless he climbed a tree. Zacchaeus would have been satisfied simply to catch a glimpse of the great Teacher. But Jesus stopped, turned, and looked directly at him. In that moment Zacchaeus was oblivious to the crowd around him. Thus began a special time with Jesus that radically changed his life (see Luke 19:1-10).

Jesus relates to you in ways that are unique to you. He knows your past; He knows what you'll face in the future. Because He knows everything about you, His word to you will perfectly fit the circumstances of your life. He knows you, and He wants you to know Him.

Therefore, you don't have to wonder what Jesus wants. If you're walking with the Lord daily, you won't have to find God's will; you'll already be in it. If you're walking with Him in obedience day by day, you'll always be in His will. The Holy Spirit's role is to guide you step by step to do God's will. Walking closely with God each day guarantees that you'll be exactly where He wants you to be. You'd have to reject all of the Holy Spirit's activity in your life to get out of the will of God.

The disciples never had to ask Jesus where they should go next. They simply looked to see where Jesus was going and stayed close to Him. Jesus was their Way (see John 14:6). They didn't need a map as long as they had Jesus. Too often we'd prefer a road map of our future rather than a relationship with the Way. It often seems easier to follow a plan than to cultivate a relationship.

We can become more concerned with our future than we are with walking intimately with God today. But Jesus will never give you a substitute for Himself. He's the only Way to the Father. That's why it's critical that you clearly know when God is speaking to you (see Isa. 30:21). If you're disoriented to how God speaks, you won't understand when He's giving you a new revelation about what He's doing. If you want to know God's will, take time to cultivate your relationship with Jesus and learn to identify His voice. He's more than willing to show you the way.

What fear do you have that only Jesus could know?

Why is it important to know that God is all-knowing and all-powerful? Why is it equally important to know that He cares for you personally?

Honestly, which do you desire more: to know what your future holds or to trust God more fully? How is knowing the Way (Jesus) better than having a road map for your life?

What was the most meaningful statement or Scripture you read today?

Reword the statement or Scripture into a prayer of response to God.

What does God want you to do in response to today's study?

How Am I Experiencing God?

Use this space to journal about your experience with God,
in particular Reality 2: God pursues a continuing love
relationship with you that is real and personal.

GROUP SESSION—REALITY 2
GOD PURSUES A CONTINUING LOVE RELATIONSHIP WITH YOU THAT IS REAL AND PERSONAL

START

Start with review and prayer. Ask volunteers to summarize the truths discussed last week in the study of Exodus 1–2.

Ask God to open everyone's heart and mind to the real, personal nature of His love for each person in the group.

READ & RESPOND

Transition to a study of the biblical text and Reality 2. Read aloud Exodus 3:1-6.

Use the following questions to discuss examples of Reality 2 in Exodus 3:1-6. (Refer to p. 35 for an overview of Reality 2, if needed.)

Who was pursuing whom in this passage? Explain your answer.

What was Moses doing when the Lord appeared to him (see v. 1)? Why is this a significant detail in understanding a relationship with God?

How did God introduce Himself to Moses (see v. 6)?

How does the genealogy in verse 6 exemplify the continuing nature of a love relationship with God?

What other evidence in this text shows that God is both real and personal?

How did Moses respond to God's presence (note each action in vv. 3-6)?

How did Moses model a proper response in relating to God?

REVIEW

Continue the discussion on a personal level by connecting themes from the daily reading with Reality 2. (Allow these questions to serve as a guide, but feel free to discuss any meaningful statements from or actions taken in response to the daily reading.)

Day 1

On a scale of 1 to 10 (1 = dead or nonexistent; 10 = vibrant and growing), how would you describe your relationship with God?

What distracts your attention from a growing relationship with God?

How do you remind yourself to live with a sense of holy expectation in order to experience God and strengthen your relationship with Him?

Day 2

Before this week's study, what word would you have used to describe the Christian life?

How has your view of life in relationship with God changed after studying Reality 2 and the life of Moses?

Day 3

How does the word *father* help you better understand the character of God and what it means to be in a relationship with Him?

How have you experienced the Heavenly Father drawing your heart toward Jesus?

Day 4

When do you have the hardest time accepting the fact that God loves you? Why is it hard to feel loved by God? When is it easiest to believe that He loves you?

Day 5

Why is it important to know that God is all-knowing and all-powerful? Why is it equally important to know that He cares for you personally?

How have you been encouraged this week in regard to your personal relationship with God?

EXPERIENCING GOD STORIES

Use this opportunity to share ways you've experienced God.

How have you experienced God this past week?

When and how did God interrupt your life in His pursuit of a continuing love relationship with you that is real and personal?

WRAP UP

Conclude the session by reading this final thought and then closing in prayer.

A love relationship with God is both extremely personal and practical. This is probably the most important factor in knowing and doing the will of God. If your love relationship with God isn't as it should be, nothing else will be in order. It's essential that you're in a right relationship with God through Jesus Christ.

Next week we'll discuss Reality 3: God invites you to become involved with Him in His work.

REALITY 3
INVITATION

God invites you to become involved with Him in His work.

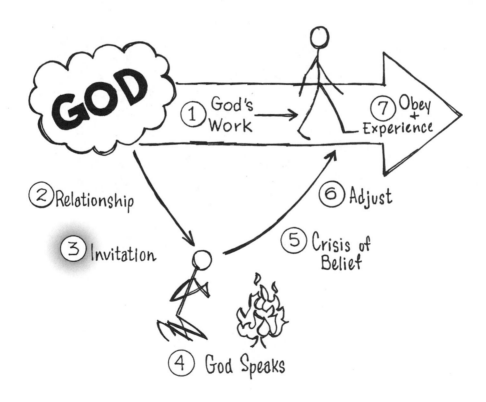

God is the sovereign Ruler of the universe. He's been working throughout history to accomplish His purposes. He doesn't ask you to dream your dreams for Him. He doesn't ask you to do your best or try your hardest for Him. He doesn't invite you to set magnificent goals and then pray He will help you achieve them.

God already has His own agenda when He approaches you. Let both of those truths sink in. God, the infinitely wise Lord of all creation, already has a plan. The almighty King of kings approaches you. He's chosen to personally interact with you, His creation, to participate in His work.

His desire is to get you from where you are to where He's working. He leads you from being self-centered to being God-centered. When God reveals to you where He's working, that becomes His invitation to join Him in His activity. When God reveals His work to you, that's the time to respond to Him.

In Moses' story God's purpose was to rescue the Israelites from slavery in Egypt and to establish them as a nation in their own land. Moses was the one through whom God intended to accomplish His plans. God invited Moses to become involved with Him in His work.

It would never have crossed Moses' mind to do something like this if God hadn't invited Him. Yet suddenly Moses was being summoned to join in a work that God had been preparing centuries for.

day 1
A PURE HEART

"Can I not do with you, Israel, as this potter
does?" declares the LORD. "Like clay in the hand
of the potter, so are you in my hand, Israel."
JEREMIAH 18:6

God knows how to bring salvation to your family, your friends, your community, and your world. Accordingly, He looks for people who will allow Him to shape them into the instruments He requires to do His divine work. Clay has no plans of its own, no aspirations for service, no reluctance to perform its given task. It's just clay—moldable, pliable, totally submissive to the will of its master.

At times we excitedly announce to God, "I've discovered my strengths and gifts, and now I know how I can best serve You!" At other times we inform Him, "I'm aware of what my weaknesses are, so I know which tasks I'm not capable of doing for You." Yet such conclusions aren't characteristic of clay. God isn't limited to working with our strengths (see 2 Cor. 12:9-10). He can mold us into whatever instrument He requires. When God's assignment demands humility, he finds a servant willing to be humbled. When His work requires zeal, He looks for someone He can fill with His Spirit. God uses holy vessels, so He finds those who will allow Him to remove their impurities.

It takes a pure heart to see God (see Matt. 5:8). You can attend church services, read your Bible, and pray, but if sin fills your heart, you won't see God. Take Isaiah, for instance. He was concerned with the death of King Uzziah, the king of Judah, but was disoriented to his Heavenly King. Then something happened that changed Isaiah's life forever.

God, in all His awesome majesty, appeared to Isaiah in the temple, surrounded by heavenly creatures. Instantly, God's presence made Isaiah aware of his sinfulness. One of the seraphim came to him with a burning coal and cleansed Isaiah of his sin. Immediately, Isaiah began to hear things he had never heard before. Now he became aware of a conversation in heaven about who might be worthy to be God's messenger to the people. This prompted Isaiah's eager response: "Here am I! Send me!" (Isa. 6:8).

Now that God had cleansed Isaiah, he was aware of heavenly concerns and was prepared to offer himself in God's service. Whereas Isaiah had been preoccupied with earthly matters, now his only concern was the activity of God.

If you've become estranged from God and His activity, you need to experience His cleansing. Sanctification prepares you to see and hear God. It enables you to serve Him. Only God can purify your heart. Allow Him to remove any impurities that hinder your relationship with Him, and then your service to Him will have meaning as you offer your life as clay in His hands to do with as He pleases.

It's not a noble task being clay. There's no glamour to it, nothing worthy of boasting, except that it's exactly what Almighty God is looking for: compliant, moldable, yielded clay.

If your tendency is to tell the Father what you can and can't do for Him, submit to His agenda and allow Him to shape you into the person He wants you to be. Like clay.

How are you resisting God's hand as it works to shape you to look more like Jesus? What impurities need to be removed from your heart?

How do you desire to see God work in the lives of people around you? How might He be shaping you as a tool for His divine work?

How is trusting God's plan for your life better than pursuing your own plan? How will you submit to His loving work in your life?

What was the most meaningful statement or Scripture you read today?

Reword the statement or Scripture into a prayer of response to God.

What does God want you to do in response to today's study?

MAY GOD RULE IN OUR MIDST

Your kingdom come,
your will be done,
on earth as it is in heaven.
MATTHEW 6:10

In heaven God's will is the only priority. A word from God brings angels to do His bidding, immediately and without question. Jesus instructed us to pray that God would accomplish His will in our world in the same way. This means God's purposes would be preeminent in our homes, our businesses, our schools, our churches, and our governments.

Jesus taught His disciples to pray that God's purposes would be carried out in the world around them. In modeling how they should pray, Jesus was teaching His disciples how to align their hearts with God's.

Jesus demonstrated this desire again at Gethsemane when He prayed, "Yet not as I will, but as you will" (Matt. 26:39). As we seek God's kingdom on earth, not our own purposes, we gain the same mind as our Heavenly Father.

As you spend intimate time with God and allow Him to show you your situation from His perspective, you'll begin to see things as God sees them. As you adjust yourself to God, your heart will begin to desire the same things God's heart desires. When you pray, you'll find yourself asking for the very things God desires (see Ps. 37:4). Matters foremost on God's heart will be preeminent in yours. Your first request in prayer won't be for yourself but for God's name to be exalted and His kingdom to be extended (see Matt. 6:9-10).

Have you been asking God to give you the desires of your heart without first seeking to understand what's on His heart? God places this important require-ment on the prayers of His children: that we seek His priorities and make them our own. This great qualifier prevents us from asking from selfishness. As we find joy in the Lord, we'll see what's truly important, and we'll long for these things as the Father does.

We become colaborers with God by faithfully praying in agreement with His desires. As you seek the Lord's will, He will guide your praying. He will invite you not only to pray but also to become involved in His activity as He answers your prayer. If He places a burden on you to pray for an individual's salvation, that burden is also His invitation to join His activity in that person's life.

Prayer prepares you to be a servant through whom God can bring about His will on earth. Pray that the Lord's absolute rule on earth will begin in your life. Then watch to see how God uses you to extend His lordship to others.

If someone closely watched your life—your words; activities; reactions; and the ways you spend your time, energy, and resources—what would they determine is most important to you?

What dominates your thought life?

What do your priorities and thoughts reveal about your will in relation to God's will?

In what current situation do you need your perspective and desire to be realigned with God's heart?

What was the most meaningful statement or Scripture you read today?

Reword the statement or Scripture into a prayer of response to God.

What does God want you to do in response to today's study?

day 3

TRUTH IS TO BE EXPERIENCED

When he had finished speaking, he said to Simon, "Put out into deep water, and let down the nets for a catch."

LUKE 5:4

When Christ teaches you something about Himself, He incorporates it into your life through experience. As the crowds gathered around, Jesus chose to board Peter's boat and teach the people from there. All day long Peter sat in the boat listening to Jesus teach the multitudes. At the close of His discourse, Jesus allowed Peter to experience the reality of what He had just been teaching the crowd. The crowd had heard the truth, but Peter was to experience it.

Jesus put His teaching into language a fisherman could understand. He told Peter to put out his nets into deep water. Peter hesitated: "Master, we have worked hard all night and haven't caught anything" (Luke 5:5). He was tired. He probably wasn't expecting a dramatic encounter with God at a time like that. Yet as Peter obeyed Jesus, he pulled in such a miraculous catch of fish that his boat almost sank. Filled with amazement, Peter recognized that he had just experienced the power of God (see v. 8). He learned that with a command from Jesus, he could do anything. In this way Jesus reordered Peter's priorities from catching fish to catching men (see v. 10). Peter's obedience led to a dramatic new insight into the person of Jesus. This experience was an invitation for Peter to walk with Jesus in an even more intimate and powerful way.

Walking with Jesus is essential. Nowhere does the Bible teach that God gives you a life plan and then abandons you to work it out. Rather, the pattern and emphasis in Scripture is a daily walk with Him in which He gives new assignments and then works through you to accomplish them.

That's what a spiritual gift is: a supernatural empowering to accomplish the assignment God gives you. Fishing was a natural skill Peter had developed. Fishing for men was a spiritual gift Jesus gave to him. Jesus was teaching Peter about God's activity and was equipping him to join the work.

So while the Lord teaches in language you can understand, don't focus on your talents, abilities, and interests to determine God's will. Instead, seek God's will and watch Him equip you for whatever assignment He gives. Pay attention to what He's teaching you through experience. He's showing you that you can join Him in His work.

God doesn't want you to merely gain intellectual knowledge of truth. He wants you to experience His truth. There are things about Jesus you'll learn only as you obey Him. Your obedience will then lead to greater revelation and opportunities for service.

What important truth about God or living in relationship with Him could you articulate by using a metaphor or an example from a favorite hobby or a common activity in your daily life?

When have you thought you understood something until you tried to do it? Similarly, when have you better understood God after experiencing something, even through mistakes or hard lessons?

What has Jesus been teaching you through experience lately? If the answer isn't immediately obvious, consider great joys or frustrations and what those reveal about Jesus, yourself, and your relationship with God.

What was the most meaningful statement or Scripture you read today?

Reword the statement or Scripture into a prayer of response to God.

What does God want you to do in response to today's study?

GOD'S REVELATION IS HIS INVITATION

> Surely the Sovereign Lord does nothing without
> revealing his plan to his servants the prophets.
> AMOS 3:7

Christians spend much time talking about seeking God's will, as though it were hidden and difficult to find. God doesn't hide His will, so it isn't difficult to discover. We don't have to plead with God to reveal His will to us. He's more eager to reveal His will than we're willing to receive it. We sometimes ask God to do things He's already done.

The people in Amos's day became disoriented to God and His desires. God had revealed His will; the problem was that they hadn't recognized it or obeyed it. Amos declared that God does nothing in the affairs of humanity without seeking one of His servants to whom He will reveal His activity. Tragically, there are times when no one's walking closely enough with Him to be receptive to His word (see Isa. 59:16; 63:5; Ezek. 22:30-31).

Jesus walked so intimately with His Father that He was always aware of what the Father was doing around Him (see John 5:19-20). Jesus said if our eyes are pure, they'll see God and recognize His activity (see Matt. 6:22). If we aren't seeing God's activity, the problem isn't a lack of revelation. The problem is that our sin prevents us from noticing it.

When God's working in someone's life, He may reveal His activity to you. That revelation is His invitation for you to join Him in His redemptive work. Be alert to God's activity around you. He will reveal His activity to His servants. If your spiritual eyes are pure, you'll be overwhelmed by all you see God doing around you.

The world operates by vision. God's people live by revelation. The world seeks grand, noble purposes and goals to achieve. People dream up the greatest and most satisfying things in which they can invest their lives. Institutions establish goals and objectives and then organize themselves to achieve them. God's people function in a radically different way. Christians arrange their lives based on the revelation of God, regardless of whether it makes sense to them.

God doesn't ask for our opinions about what's best for our future, our family, our church, or our country. He already knows. God wants to get the attention of His people and reveal to us what is on His heart and what is His will, for God's ways are not our ways (see Isa. 55:8-9).

When people don't base their lives on God's revelation, they "cast off restraint" (Prov. 29:18). That is, they do what's right in their own eyes. They set their goals, arrange their agendas, and then pray for God's blessings. Some Christians are living far outside the will of God, yet they have the audacity to pray and ask God to bless their efforts.

The only way you can know God's will is for Him to reveal it to you. You'll never discover it on your own. When you hear from the Father, you have an immediate agenda for your life: obedience. As the writer of Proverbs observed, "Blessed is the one who heeds wisdom's instruction" (29:18).

When have you worried about knowing God's will? What were you actually doing to discern His will? What was the result?

What sin is clouding your spiritual vision?

In what areas are you currently living according to your own agenda—even asking God to bless your efforts—instead of seeking to join Him?

What was the most meaningful statement or Scripture you read today?

Reword the statement or Scripture into a prayer of response to God.

What does God want you to do in response to today's study?

NOW IS THE ACCEPTABLE TIME

*Another disciple said to him, "Lord,
first let me go and bury my father."*
MATTHEW 8:21

Often our struggle as Christians isn't in deciding whether we should obey Christ but in whether we'll obey immediately. God's timing is perfect. When He speaks, the time to respond in obedience is now. We often act as if we have all the time in the world to obey Him, but history doesn't wait on our commitments. There's no such thing as postponing a decision with God. Either we obey or we disobey. It's either faith or unbelief, obedience or disobedience. God's revelation of His will is His invitation to respond immediately.

Some would-be disciples pledged their willingness to follow Jesus, but they told Him they weren't ready yet. In Jesus' day a Jewish man was expected to care for his elderly parents until they died. One man wanted to wait until his father died before going with Jesus. This would be an honorable delay. The man had to choose between this important responsibility and heeding a call from the Lord. Yet God knew this man, and He knew the man's father. God would have taken care of the man's father if only he had followed Jesus. This was an opportunity to walk with the Son of God, yet the concerns of this life were competing for priority with obedience to God.

Timing our obedience is crucial. Invitations from God come with a limited opportunity to respond. Some opportunities to serve Him, if not accepted immediately, will be lost. Occasions to minister to others may pass us by. When God invites us to intercede for someone, it may be critical that we stop what we're doing and immediately adjust our lives to what God's doing.

Missing opportunities to serve the Lord can be tragic. When an invitation comes from God, the time to respond is now. That's why Scripture tells us God is concerned with our heart. If we don't keep our heart in love with Jesus, we'll be prone to disobey when God speaks to us. And our disobedience could affect the lives of others.

God's timing is always perfect. He knows you, and He's fully aware of your circumstances. He knows all He's built into your life until now, and He extends His invitation knowing His resources are more than adequate for any assignment He gives you.

When God speaks, it's always from the context of eternity. We don't have to know all the implications of what He's asking. We just have to know that it's a word from Almighty God. Now is always the acceptable time to respond to the Lord.

In what area of life have you been postponing a decision about an invitation from God? Why haven't you responded? What does this inaction reveal?

Because delayed obedience is choosing to be disobedient, how does your inaction affect your relationship with God?

Why is timing significant in obeying God? Identify as many factors, positive or negative, that may be affected by your obedience.

What was the most meaningful statement or Scripture you read today?

Reword the statement or Scripture into a prayer of response to God.

What does God want you to do in response to today's study?

How Am I Experiencing God?

Use this space to journal about your experience with God, in particular
Reality 3: God invites you to become involved with Him in His work.

GROUP SESSION—REALITY 3
GOD INVITES YOU TO BECOME INVOLVED WITH HIM IN HIS WORK

START

Start with review and prayer. Ask volunteers to summarize the truths discussed last week in the study of Exodus 3:1-6.

Thank God for pursuing a relationship with you. Ask God to make each person's heart responsive to His invitation to become involved with Him in His work.

READ & RESPOND

Transition to a study of the biblical text and Reality 3. Read aloud Exodus 3:7-10.

Use the following questions to discuss examples of Reality 3 in Exodus 3:7-10. (Refer to p. 53 for an overview of Reality 3, if needed.)

What need did God identify (see v. 7)?

What work was God doing (see v. 8)?

What were some of the details God didn't reveal to Moses at this time?

Why do you think God didn't give Moses all the details at the front end of the assignment (see vv. 9-10)?

How did God invite Moses to become involved with Him in His work?

Why is it significant that God phrased His invitation to join His work as an instruction rather than as a request?

How does God's use of a command deepen your understanding of what it means to be involved in His work?

REVIEW

Continue the discussion on a personal level by connecting themes from the daily reading with Reality 3. (Allow these questions to serve as a guide, but feel free to discuss any meaningful statements from or actions taken in response to the daily reading.)

Day 1

How do you desire to see God work in the lives of people around you?

How might God be shaping you as a tool for His divine work?

How is trusting God's plan for your life better than pursuing your own plan? How will you submit to His loving work in your life?

Day 2

In what current situation do you need your perspective and desire to be realigned with God's heart?

Day 3

Moses experienced God in a brand-new way as God was inviting Moses to join His work. What has Jesus been teaching you through experience lately? If the answer isn't immediately obvious, consider great joys or frustrations and what those reveal about Jesus, yourself, and your relationship with God.

Day 4

When have you worried about knowing God's will? What were you actually doing to discern His will? What was the result?

In what areas are you currently living according to your own agenda—even asking God to bless your efforts—instead of seeking to join Him?

Day 5

In what area of life have you been postponing a decision about an invitation from God? Why haven't you responded? What does this inaction reveal?

Because delayed obedience is choosing to be disobedient, how does your inaction affect your relationship with God?

Why is timing significant in obeying God? Identify as many factors, positive or negative, that may be affected by your obedience.

EXPERIENCING GOD STORIES

Use this opportunity to share ways you've experienced God.

How have you experienced God this past week?

When, where, or how has God invited you to join Him in His work?

Why is it important to remember that it's God's work, not yours alone?

WRAP UP

Conclude the session by reading this final thought and then closing in prayer.

When God reveals to you where He's working,
that's His invitation to join Him in His activity.
The revelation is the invitation. If He's made
something known to you, it's time to respond.

Next week we'll discuss Reality 4: God speaks by the Holy
Spirit through the Bible, prayer, circumstances, and the
church to reveal Himself, His purposes, and His ways.

GOD SPEAKS

God speaks by the Holy Spirit through the Bible,
prayer, circumstances, and the church to reveal
Himself, His purposes, and His ways.

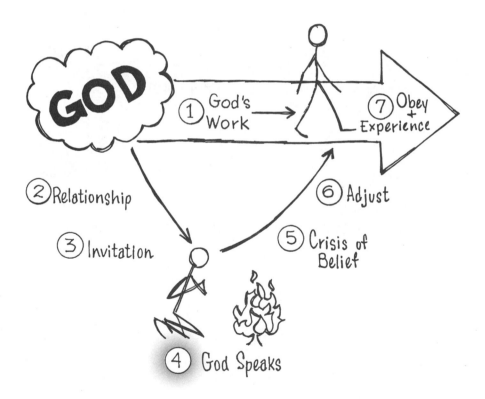

The testimony of the Bible, from Genesis to Revelation, is that God speaks to His people. In our day God communicates to us through the Holy Spirit. The Spirit uses the Bible, prayer, circumstances, and the church (other believers) to guide us. When you hear God speak to you through a verse of Scripture, it's always best to verify what you've heard through prayer, other believers, and your circumstances. If you hear God say the same thing through each of these sources, you can proceed confidently.

God draws you into a deeper and closer walk with Him so that you can trust Him and have faith in Him. He will reveal His purposes to you so that you can become involved in His work rather than merely pursuing your own goals and dreams. He reveals His ways so that you can accomplish His purposes in a manner that glorifies Him. God's ways are not our ways (see Isa. 55:8-9). You can't discover these truths about God on your own. Divine truth must be revealed.

God came and talked to Moses about His will. He wanted Moses to go to Egypt to deliver the Israelites. He revealed to Moses His holiness, His mercy, His power, His name, and His purpose to keep His promise to Abraham and to give Israel the promised land.

When God spoke, Moses knew it was God. He knew what God said. And he knew what he had to do in response. This pattern works the same for you today. When God speaks, you'll know it's God. You'll know what He's saying. And you'll know what God wants you to do.

GOD SPEAKS IN MANY POWERFUL WAYS

In the past God spoke to our ancestors through the prophets at many times and in various ways, but in these last days he has spoken to us by his Son.
HEBREWS 1:1-2

Our generation is preoccupied with methods. When we find a program that works in one business, we immediately want to package and distribute it so that it will work for others. This attitude carries over into the spiritual life as well. We spend much energy looking for spiritual disciplines, books, seminars, or conferences that work in order to feel satisfied with our Christian life. But God doesn't want us to trust in methods. He wants us to trust in Him.

Trusting in methods rather than in a Person seriously limits the way we experience God. When we expect Him to speak to us only in predictable ways, we forget that God is much more complex than our perception of Him. In times past, God spoke in dreams and visions. He used nature, miraculous signs, prophets, "a gentle whisper" (1 Kings 19:12), fire, trumpets, fleece, the casting of lots, and angels. He spoke in the middle of the night, during worship services, at mealtimes, during funerals, while people were walking along the road, through sermons, in the middle of a storm, and through His Son. The important thing wasn't the way God communicated but the fact that He spoke. The means God uses to communicate with us is irrelevant; the fact that He's communicating is what's critical.

Have you lost your sense of awe that the Creator still chooses to speak to you, His creation? Do you approach the reading of your Bible with a holy expectation, listening for the life-changing words God has for you that day?

God's word is powerful. When God speaks, nothing remains the same. At the beginning of time God spoke, and a universe was created from nothing. God followed a pattern when He created the earth: He spoke; it was so; it was good (see Gen. 1:3-4). This pattern continued throughout the Bible. Whenever God revealed His plans, things happened just as He said, and God considered the result good (see Phil. 2:13). God doesn't make suggestions. He speaks with the full determination to see that what He has said will come to fruition.

Whenever Jesus spoke, what He said came to pass. Lepers found that a word from Jesus meant healing (see Luke 5:13; 17:14). A blind man discovered that a word from Jesus meant sight (see Luke 18:42). Through a barren fig tree the disciples saw that a curse from Jesus meant destruction (see Mark 11:14,20). A sinner experienced forgiveness through a word from Jesus (see John 8:11).

How many attempts did it take Jesus to raise Lazarus from the dead? Only one (see John 11:43-44). There was never a time Jesus spoke when what He said didn't happen.

How powerful a word from God is to your life! As you read your Bible and pray, listen to what God has to say to you about His will for you. Don't limit yourself to a method, expecting to hear from your Father only in predictable ways. Rather, open yourself up to other means by which God wants to commune with you. As you're receptive to His voice, you'll experience Him in entirely new dimensions (see Isa. 55:10-11).

In what ways have you experienced God's voice in the past?

How have you trusted in methods rather than in a Person, expecting God to speak only in certain ways?

When was the most recent time you were in awe of God's speaking to you?

What was the most meaningful statement or Scripture you read today?

Reword the statement or Scripture into a prayer of response to God.

What does God want you to do in response to today's study?

day 2
THE BIBLE

All Scripture is God-breathed and is useful for
teaching, rebuking, correcting and training in
righteousness, so that the servant of God may be
thoroughly equipped for every good work.
2 TIMOTHY 3:16-17

All Scripture is useful. Knowing this, we cheat ourselves when we don't access every book, every truth, every verse, and every page of our Bibles for the promises and commands God has for us. Because every verse of Scripture is inspired by God and gainful to us, we shouldn't pick and choose which verses we'll read and study. We shouldn't claim verses we like and ignore those that convict us. If we're to become mature disciples of Jesus, we must allow every Scripture to speak to us and teach us what God desires for us to learn.

If you aren't firmly grounded in God's Word, you'll be bombarded with an assortment of doctrines, lifestyles, and behaviors, and you'll have no means to evaluate whether they're approved by God. Scripture enables us to evaluate the soundness of doctrines that are being taught. Scripture ought to be the basis of any reproof or correction we bring to another person.

You can't develop a righteous life apart from God's Word. Righteousness must be cultivated. As you fill your mind with the words of God and as you obey His instructions, He will guide you in the ways of righteousness. Scripture will equip you for any good work God calls you to do. If you feel inadequate for a task God has given you, search the Scriptures, for within them you'll find the wisdom you need to carry out His assignment. Allow the Word of God to permeate, guide, and enrich your life.

So why wouldn't you be eager to spend time in God's Word? Is it because what you read makes you uneasy? When you listen to sermons, do the Scriptures seem aimed directly at you? Believe it or not, that's a good thing. You're experiencing the reality that the Word of God is alive and can read your thoughts and judge your intentions.

When God's Word speaks to you, it's always for a purpose. God knows your heart and knows what you need to do to bring your life into conformity with Christ. If you have a problem with sinful talk, the word that comes to you will address the tongue. If you're struggling to forgive, God's Word will confront you with His standard for forgiveness. If pride has a stronghold in your life, God's Word will speak to you about humility. Whatever sin needs to be addressed, you'll be confronted by God's Word on the matter.

One way you can escape the discomfort of conviction is to avoid hearing God speak to you. You may neglect reading your Bible and stay away from places where it's taught. You may avoid those who you know will uphold the truths of Scripture. The best response, however, is to pray as the psalmist did: "Search me, God, and know my heart" (Ps. 139:23). Regularly allow the Word of God to wash over you and find any sin or impurity (see Eph. 5:26). Always make the connection between your life and what God's saying to you through His Word. Make a habit of taking the Word of God seriously, knowing it's capable of judging your heart and mind.

What time do you regularly set aside to listen to God through His Word?

What was the most recent matter you felt convicted about when reading the Bible?

How did you respond to that discomfort?

What was the most meaningful statement or Scripture you read today?

Reword the statement or Scripture into a prayer of response to God.

What does God want you to do in response to today's study?

day 3
PRAYER

Do not be like them, for your Father knows
what you need before you ask him.
MATTHEW 6:8

Prayer doesn't give you spiritual power. That may sound surprising, but it's true. Prayer doesn't give you power. It aligns your life with God so that He chooses to demonstrate His power through you. The purpose of prayer isn't to convince God to change your circumstances but to prepare you to be involved in God's activity. The fervent prayer of the people at Pentecost didn't induce the Holy Spirit to come on them. Prayer brought them to a place where they were ready to participate in the mighty work God had already planned.

Jesus told His followers to remain in Jerusalem until the Spirit came on them (see Acts 1:4-5). The disciples obeyed His command, waiting for God's next directive. As they prayed, God adjusted their lives to what He intended to do next. As they prayed, a unity developed among them. For the first time the disciples used Scripture as their guide in decision making (see vv. 15-26). The day of Pentecost arrived, and the city of Jerusalem filled with pilgrims from around the world. When God released His Holy Spirit on the disciples, He had already filled the city with messengers who would carry the gospel to every nation. Prayer had prepared the disciples for their obedient response.

Prayer is designed to adjust you to God's will, not to adjust God to your will. If God hasn't responded to what you're praying, you may need to adjust your praying to align with God's agenda. Rather than focusing on what you'd like to happen, realize God may be more concerned with what He wants to happen in you.

Consider that even before you call on Him, the Father has already begun to provide all you need (see Isa. 65:24). Jesus wanted His disciples to learn how intimately God knew and loved each of them. That's why He told them to pray. He assured them that even before they prayed, God knew all about their situation.

Prayer isn't designed for us to inform God of our needs, for He already knows them. Why, then, should we pray? Prayer enables us to experience God more intimately. The more a child experiences the loving provision of a parent, the more convinced he or she becomes of his parent's unrelenting love. Often a parent anticipates a child's need before the child recognizes it and prepares in advance to provide for that need. Likewise, our Heavenly Father knows exactly what we'll face today and next week. He's eager for us to experience Him as He provides for us.

To our surprise, we often discover that God knows far better than we do what's best for us. At times we assume that we know what would benefit us. We can even be foolish enough to assume we don't require anything of God. Yet God wants us to go to Him in our need (see Matt. 7:7). He's ready to show His strength through our weakness. Our Heavenly Father knows exactly what's best for us, and He's prepared to provide for every need if we will only ask (see Phil. 4:13).

What have you been praying for recently? What needs do you have?

What answers to prayer have you experienced?

When have you been aware of God's changing you through prayer?

What was the most meaningful statement or Scripture you read today?

Reword the statement or Scripture into a prayer of response to God.

What does God want you to do in response to today's study?

day 4
CIRCUMSTANCES

When the Lord saw that he had gone over to look,
God called to him from within the bush, "Moses!
Moses!" And Moses said, "Here I am."
EXODUS 3:4

Christians habitually seek God's voice through prayer, through His Word, or through His messengers. Yet sometimes we fail to hear God speak through His activity, even though He's working all around us. God encourages His people to watch for His activity so that they'll know how they should respond and adjust their lives.

Moses was going through the routine of his day when he noticed an ordinary thing: a burning bush. Moses also noticed something extraordinary. Although the bush was burning, it wasn't being consumed. Moses turned aside to look more closely.

When the Lord saw Moses turning aside from the routine of his day, He spoke to him. Everything God had been doing for 40 years in Moses' life was culminating in this moment. Much of God's redemptive plan waited for Moses to notice the uncommon in the midst of the common.

There will be times when, immersed in the ordinary details of life, you may be oblivious to something extraordinary that's right next to you. You can be in the midst of a common moment, except this time the activity is filled with the presence of God. There may be times when, in the middle of your harried day, you notice something unusual. Your first reaction might be "I'm too tired to go aside to investigate this!" or "I'm not going to disrupt my life for this." Yet in that moment you may have the opportunity for a unique encounter with God.

Often God doesn't speak while you're worshiping at church but in the ordinary experiences of life. Many of God's most profound and history-changing encounters come during those ordinary experiences. When you see the unusual in the midst of the mundane, don't continue business as usual. It may be that God has ordained that moment to be a life-changing time for you and those around you. To people with spiritual discernment, God's activity is a significant revelation about His heart and His will.

If you're sensitive to what God is doing around you, He will clearly speak to you through His activity. You'll know that God is at work, because what you see will astound you, and human power and wisdom will not explain it. When you experience events that surpass your understanding and ability, it may be that God is communicating a critical message to you.

If you want to hear God's voice, look around you to see what He's doing. When you're watching for God at work, what you see will reveal His character, and you'll have a fresh understanding of how to respond to Him.

In what ways have you experienced God's extraordinary presence?

When has God radically changed the direction of your life through a seemingly ordinary circumstance?

Consider your current circumstances. What unusual details should you investigate to learn whether God is making you aware of His activity?

What was the most meaningful statement or Scripture you read today?

Reword the statement or Scripture into a prayer of response to God.

What does God want you to do in response to today's study?

day 5
IF GOD SEEMS SILENT

"The days are coming," declares the Sovereign LORD,
"when I will send a famine through the land—
not a famine of food or a thirst for water,
but a famine of hearing the words of the LORD."
AMOS 8:11

One more way God communicates that you might not expect is through silence. The Israelites blatantly ignored and rejected God's Word to them, and God responded by sending a famine. This famine was far more severe than a shortage of food and water. Instead, they were deprived of His words of life.

God's silence may be hardly noticeable at first. You may still remember times when God spoke to you, but you gradually realize you haven't heard His voice for a long time. If you realize you're in a drought, immediately seek God and ask what adjustments He requires for your life so that you can once again enjoy fellowship with Him. Maybe you disobeyed His previous instructions to you, and He's waiting on your obedience before giving you a new direction. It may be that there's unconfessed sin in your life or that you have a damaged relationship with someone (see Isa. 1:15; 1 Pet. 3:7). It's possible that you've done too much talking in your prayer times and that He wants you to listen. God's silences can be powerful times for Him to communicate with you.

God is God! Because He's God, He expects a listening ear and an eager response when He speaks. He won't be mocked (see Gal. 6:7). Take Jonah, for example. He didn't like the assignment God gave him. God directed him to leave his homeland and go to the enemy city of Nineveh, a hostile and evil center of idol worship. There Jonah was to warn the people of God's impending judgment and urge them to repent.

The Hebrews hated the people of Nineveh, so the rebellious prophet fled in the opposite direction, hoping for a different word from God that was more to his liking. Instead, God was determined that his word to Jonah would be obeyed (see Isa. 55:10-11). When He spoke to Jonah again, His second message was the same as the first. However, during the interval, Jonah had been buffeted by storms and had traveled in the stomach of a fish for three days. This time he was prepared to hear God and do His bidding.

God also spoke to the prophet Jeremiah two times (see Jer. 33:1-3). But Jeremiah accepted God's Word to him the first time. The second time God spoke gave Jeremiah a fuller revelation of what He'd first told him.

What God says to us next will depend on how we responded to His previous word to us. If, like Jonah, we disobeyed His earlier instructions, God will give them a second time. If we obeyed His first directive, as Jeremiah did, He will give us a fresh and deeper expression of His will (see Matt. 25:23).

If you haven't received a fresh word from God, return to the previous directive God told you and examine your obedience. Is the Lord still waiting for your obedience? Seek to be like Jeremiah. Properly respond to your Lord's instructions the first time.

When was the most recent time you knew God was speaking to you?

What was the most recent thing God revealed to you?

How did you respond to God's direction?

What was the most meaningful statement or Scripture you read today?

Reword the statement or Scripture into a prayer of response to God.

What does God want you to do in response to today's study?

How Am I Experiencing God?

Use this space to journal about your experience with God, in particular
Reality 4: God speaks by the Holy Spirit through the Bible, prayer,
circumstances, and the church to reveal Himself, His purposes, and His ways.

GROUP SESSION—REALITY 4
GOD SPEAKS BY THE HOLY SPIRIT THROUGH THE BIBLE, PRAYER, CIRCUMSTANCES, AND THE CHURCH TO REVEAL HIMSELF, HIS PURPOSES, AND HIS WAYS

START

Start with review and prayer. Ask volunteers to summarize the truths discussed last week in the study of Exodus 3:7-10.

Ask God to speak clearly during this time together to reveal Himself, His purposes, and His ways in your lives.

READ & RESPOND

Transition to a study of the biblical text and Reality 4. Explain that today's reading will include the verses from the past two sessions to provide the full context for the conversation between God and Moses.

Read aloud Exodus 3:1-22.

Use the following questions to discuss examples of Reality 4 in Exodus 3:1-22. (Refer to p. 71 for an overview of Reality 4, if needed.)

What circumstance first drew Moses' attention to what God wanted to say to him (see vv. 2-4)?

What did God specifically reveal about Himself (see vv. 5-6,14)?

What did God specifically reveal about His purposes (see vv. 7-10)?

What did God specifically reveal about His ways for accomplishing those purposes (see vv. 12,15-22)?

What evidence do you see in this passage that God spoke clearly and specifically to Moses, not just in vague feelings or interests?

REVIEW

Continue the discussion on a personal level by connecting themes from the daily reading with Reality 4. (Allow these questions to serve as a guide, but feel free to discuss any meaningful statements from or actions taken in response to the daily reading.)

Day 1

In what ways have you experienced God's voice in the past?

How have you trusted in methods rather than in a Person, expecting God to speak only in certain ways?

Day 2

What time do you regularly set aside to listen to God through His Word?

What was the most recent matter you felt convicted about when reading the Bible?

How did you respond to that discomfort?

Day 3

What have you been praying for recently?

What answers to prayer have you experienced?

When have you been aware of God's changing you through prayer?

Day 4

In what ways have you experienced God's extraordinary presence?

When has God radically changed the direction of your life through a seemingly ordinary circumstance?

Day 5

When has God seemed silent?

What did God reveal during that time of silence?

EXPERIENCING GOD STORIES

Use this opportunity to share ways you've experienced God.

How have you experienced God this past week?

When, where, or how has God spoken to you by the Holy Spirit through the Bible, prayer, circumstances, and the church?

What has God revealed about Himself, His purposes, and His ways?

WRAP UP

Conclude your time by reading this final thought and then closing in prayer.

How can you know something is from God and not just your own idea? Just like Moses, when God speaks, you'll know it's God. You'll know what He's saying. And you'll know what God wants you to do. Don't overcomplicate the voice and will of God.

Next week we'll discuss Reality 5: God's invitation for you to work with Him always leads you to a crisis of belief that requires faith and action.

CRISIS OF BELIEF

God's invitation for you to work with Him always leads you to a crisis of belief that requires faith and action.

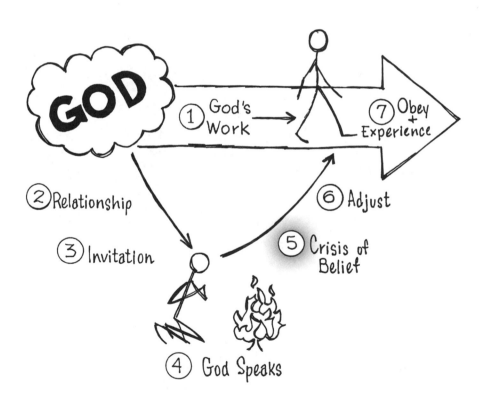

God wants a watching world to come to know who He truly is. He doesn't call you to get involved in His activity merely so that people can see what you can do. He calls you to an assignment that you can't accomplish apart from His divine intervention. God's assignments have God-sized dimensions. This doesn't mean God doesn't ask us to undertake mundane, seemingly ordinary tasks. But when God is involved in anything, there are always eternal, divine dimensions, implications, and possibilities.

When God asks you to do something you can't do, you face a crisis of belief. You have to decide what you really believe about God. Can He and will He do what He said He wants to do through you? Can God do the seemingly impossible through your ordinary life? The way you respond to His invitation reveals what you truly believe about God, regardless of what you say.

God's invitation for Moses to work with Him led to a crisis of belief that required faith and action. Moses offered God numerous objections. In each case he doubted God's power more than he questioned his own ability. God finally convinced Moses to become involved in delivering Israel from slavery (see Ex. 4:1-17).

This major turning point is where so many people miss out on experiencing God's mighty power working through them. If they can't understand exactly how everything's going to happen, they won't proceed. They want to walk with God by sight, not by faith. But to follow God, you have to walk by faith, because without faith it's impossible to please Him (see Heb. 11:6). Faith is more than just belief. Biblical faith always requires action (see Jas. 2:14-17). God doesn't want you to merely believe what He says. He wants you to obey what He commands. All God's promises and invitations will be meaningless to you unless you respond with faith and action.

day 1
SPIRITUAL WRESTLING

Watch and pray so that you will not fall into temptation.
The spirit is willing, but the flesh is weak.
MARK 14:38

Too often we settle for much less than what God wants to do through us. We read in Jeremiah 32:27, "I am the LORD, the God of all mankind. Is anything too hard for me?" and we answer, "No, Lord." Yet when we face difficult situations, we begin to qualify our belief in God and lower our expectations of what God will do.

It's one thing to believe God could perform a miracle in the Bible, a thousand years ago, or even in the life of a friend; it's quite another matter to wholeheartedly believe God can do anything He chooses to do in our lives.

When Almighty God speaks to us, what we do next proves what we believe about Him, regardless of what we say. God revealed to Moses His plan to orchestrate the greatest exodus in human history, and He wanted to use Moses to accomplish it. Yet Moses responded by arguing with God. Moses was overwhelmed by what he heard and began to make excuses for why he couldn't participate in God's activity. Moses would have readily acknowledged his belief in God's power, but he simply didn't believe God could do His miraculous work through him. Moses' argument with God limited his ministry for the rest of his life (see Ex. 4:10-16).

At times your spirit must demand supremacy over your flesh. Your spirit will know what your Lord wants you to do, but your flesh will cry out for its own comfort. There are times when even sleep must be denied, because it would be disastrous for you to rest at such a time.

When the Lord commands you to "watch and pray" (Mark 14:38), it's crucial that you obey. As Jesus prayed in the garden of Gethsemane, He knew that the pinnacle of His ministry was quickly approaching. He was aware that the legions of hell were marshaling their forces to defeat Him. If there was ever a critical time for His closest friends to undergird Him in prayer, this was it.

Jesus told them that He was deeply distressed, even to the point of death. Surely they could have sensed the intensity in His voice and the urgency of His demeanor, and surely they could have found the strength to obey His request.

Yet He found them asleep. No excuses. They'd fallen asleep at the most pivotal moment in human history, not once but three times!

Jesus asks you to join Him in what He's doing. He may ask you to watch and pray for an hour. You may have to deny your physical needs and desires in order to pray with Him. You may have to leave the comfort of your bed or your home. You may even have to sacrifice your safety to be where Jesus is. Seek to bring every physical desire under the control of the Holy Spirit so that nothing impedes your accomplishing what Jesus asks of you.

Do you sense there may be far more that God wants to do through your life than what you've been experiencing? Ask God to show you what it is. Then be prepared to respond in faith and obedience to what He tells you.

With what decision are you currently wrestling? Why?

What do your hesitations and excuses reveal about your belief in God?

How will you submit your flesh to the supremacy of your spirit?

What was the most meaningful statement or Scripture you read today?

Reword the statement or Scripture into a prayer of response to God.

What does God want you to do in response to today's study?

day 2
IT'S NOT DIFFICULT, BUT IT'S A CHOICE

*What I am commanding you today is not
too difficult for you or beyond your reach.*
DEUTERONOMY 30:11

The Christian life isn't difficult. The same Christ who lived a perfect, obedient, and sinless life stands prepared to live it again through you (see Gal. 2:20). God's will isn't hard to discern. He's given us the Scriptures, which reveal His will, and He's placed His Holy Spirit within us to guide us to His perfect will in every situation (see John 16:13). Our greatest challenge is to wholly commit our lives to follow God's will obediently as He reveals it.

Moses gathered the Israelites before they were to enter the promised land. God described what they had to do in order to obey Him, giving detailed instructions so that they wouldn't misunderstand what He expected of them. Then God asked them to make a choice. If they chose to disobey His commands, they'd face His wrath. If they chose to obey, they'd receive His blessing.

God's Word comes to you in the same way. It isn't too complex to understand. The question is, How will you respond? Nowhere in Scripture did God excuse disobedience because His instructions were too vague or complex. Condemnation always came because people knew exactly what God wanted them to do, yet they chose not to do it. God, through His Holy Spirit, always gives you sufficient revelation and strength to take the next step with Him. If you're uncertain about what God's asking of you, make sure you're obeying all you know at the present time. Through your obedience God's next instruction will become clear.

Your life is the sum of the responses you've made to God. Once God makes Himself known to you, what you do next is your decision. Your reaction reflects what you believe about Him. The rich young ruler lived a moral life. He was well versed in Scripture and in the laws of God. But his response to Jesus' invitation clearly showed that although he possessed a head knowledge of God's teachings, he didn't know God in an experiential way that could be demonstrated by a response of faith (see Matt. 19:16-22).

God's invitation for you to work with Him always leads you to a crisis of belief that requires faith and action. Anytime you hear from God, you have a choice to make. This truth can dramatically affect your prayer life. Every time you pray, you must be aware that if God answers your prayer and reveals His will to you, it will immediately require you to reorient your life. Each time you read your Bible, you must be prepared to obey what God tells you.

Why did God use Moses so significantly? And why were others, like the rich young ruler, never heard from again? Choices! Moses chose to believe, and his belief was proved by faithful action. The rich young ruler couldn't bring himself to obey, and Scripture tells us that "he went away sad" (v. 22). You're faced with the same question as the rich young ruler. Will you respond positively to Christ's invitation? Will you choose to follow Jesus, trusting Him with everything in your life? God is asking you to make a choice.

In what areas of your life have you been overcomplicating God's will or feeling confused about what He wants you to do?

What specific command in Scripture do you know you've been neglecting or failing to obey?

How can you constantly remind yourself to choose obedience to Jesus?

What was the most meaningful statement or Scripture you read today?

Reword the statement or Scripture into a prayer of response to God.

What does God want you to do in response to today's study?

day 3
HELP MY UNBELIEF!

Immediately the boy's father exclaimed,
"I do believe; help me overcome my unbelief!"
MARK 9:24

Most fear is fear of the unknown. We don't know what lies ahead of us, so we become apprehensive. Our imaginations can magnify problems until they seem insurmountable. We need a sound mind to see things in proper perspective. That's why God gave us His Holy Spirit: to enable us to see things as God sees them.

Fear is no excuse to disobey God. There's no reason to live in fear when you have the mighty presence of the Holy Spirit within you. Fear will enslave you, but Christ has come to set you free. Ask God to free you from any fear you're experiencing and to open your eyes. As He reveals the reality of your situation, He will enable you to continue in obedience.

Faith is based on reality. While fear comes from what we don't know, faith is based on what we do know. In other words, faith is trust. It's confidence in someone or something you know in the midst of what you don't know. We don't live recklessly in ignorance. Before we trust others with something precious to us, we first try to find out whether they're trustworthy.

A father came to Jesus asking to know God in such a way that he could trust Him to cure his son. His son had been possessed by an evil spirit since early childhood. The father didn't know Jesus well, but he'd heard and seen enough to convince him that if there was any hope for his son, it lay with Jesus. In desperation he cried out to Jesus for help. Jesus' response was to heal his son. The desperate father had correctly gone to Jesus with his problem even though he was struggling with his faith.

When you're struggling to believe, that's not the time to avoid Christ or to be ashamed of your struggle. You'll never increase your faith by not going to Jesus. Rather, Jesus wants to help you with your belief. Not only can He can meet your need, but He will also give you faith to trust Him to provide for you.

If you're struggling to believe God can take care of your need, it's because you don't know Him as He wants you to. Go to Him and allow Him to convince you of His ability to meet every need you'll ever face. It's by faith that God's mighty power is released into a Christian's life (see Heb. 11:32-35).

God wants to build your understanding of Him until your faith is sufficient to trust and obey Him in each situation (see Mark 9:23-25). The moment you turn to Him with a genuine commitment to rid yourself of doubt, God will match your doubt with a revelation of Himself that can convince you of His faithfulness.

When one of Jesus' own disciples struggled to believe, Jesus revealed Himself in such a way that every doubt vanished (see John 20:27-28). You can resolve your lack of faith only in God's presence. He must reveal Himself in such a way that any doubt you might have is removed. Jesus did this with His disciples (see Matt. 8:26). He involved them in a consistent, growing relationship with Himself. Jesus took them through teaching to small miracles, to large miracles, and to the resurrection. Jesus knew the redemption of the world rested on His disciples' believing Him. What does God want to do in the lives of those around you that waits on your trust in Him and the removal of your doubts?

Don't hide your doubts or questions. Give them to Jesus. How do you struggle to believe in God, God's goodness, or God's power?

Make a list of specific areas in which you're fearful or anxious. Then identify a specific need you'll give to Jesus instead of worrying about it.

What was the most meaningful statement or Scripture you read today?

Reword the statement or Scripture into a prayer of response to God.

What does God want you to do in response to today's study?

day 4
DON'T GET DISTRACTED

Peter turned and saw that the disciple whom
Jesus loved was following them. ... When Peter
saw him, he asked, "Lord, what about him?"
JOHN 21:20-21

The first thing you do after God speaks to you is critical. Jesus was telling Peter what type of ministry he'd have and what type of death he'd suffer (see John 21:18-19). It was a sacred moment in Peter's life, as his Lord pulled back the curtain to his future. His life wouldn't be easy but would nonetheless be ordained and blessed by his Lord and Master.

Rather than responding to what Jesus told him, Peter looked around at his fellow disciples. His glance fell on John, the disciple whom Jesus loved. "Lord, what about him?" Peter asked (v. 21). Peter had just been given the somber news of his future death, and his natural response was to compare his assignment with that of John. This is the great temptation of God's servants: to compare our situation with that of others. Did God give my friend a larger house? Did God heal my friend's loved one and not mine? Did God allow my friend to receive appreciation and praise for his work while I remain anonymous? Did God allow another Christian to remain close to her family while I'm far removed from mine?

Jesus assigned Peter and John to walk two different paths, but both Peter and John have enriched our lives. Jesus knew how dangerous it is when a servant takes his eyes off the master to focus on a fellow servant. The only thing that should matter to you is what God has called you to do. It doesn't matter whether His plan for someone else looks preferable or His plan for you seems difficult.

Nothing you could ever experience, no matter how terrible or frightening, could ever separate you from the love of God (see Rom 8:35-39). No tribulation and distress you might ever suffer could be so intense that God's love for you isn't even more fervent. No persecution could be so painful that God's love can't bring comfort. Famine might starve you of food, but you'll never hunger for the Father's love. Poverty can't strip you of God's compassion, just as even death itself is incapable of robbing you of your Heavenly Father's infinite love.

If you base your view of God's love on your circumstances, you'll become confused. There may be times when you'll ask, "How could a loving God allow this to happen to me?" You may begin to question what you find clearly stated in the Word of God. God promised you'll never be separated from His love; He didn't say you'll never face hardship, persecution, poverty, or danger. If you doubt that God can love you and still allow you to experience difficult experiences, consider the life of Jesus. If you allow the death of Jesus on the cross to forever settle any questions you might have about God's love, you'll approach difficult circumstances with confidence.

Knowing there will never be anything that can separate you from God's perfect love, you'll watch to see how God expresses His love in each circumstance. Don't ever judge God's love based on your circumstances or compared to other people's circumstances. Instead, evaluate your circumstances from the perspective of God's love. Where's your focus? Have you become more concerned with the way God treats someone else than with the way He relates to you?

In what specific ways have you been comparing your circumstances to other people's lives? How has comparison taken your attention off Jesus, distracted you from His work, and robbed you of His joy?

How does the promise that God's love for you is greater than even the most difficult circumstances (see Rom. 8:35-39) give you hope and confidence? How will this promise help keep you focused on Jesus instead of on your circumstances?

What was the most meaningful statement or Scripture you read today?

Reword the statement or Scripture into a prayer of response to God.

What does God want you to do in response to today's study?

day 5
GOD IS FAITHFUL

The one who calls you is faithful, and he will do it.
1 THESSALONIANS 5:24

God never calls us to do anything without faithfully keeping His Word and enabling us to do it. We aren't always faithful to do what God tells us, but He remains faithful and stands by His Word to fulfill what He's promised (see Isa. 46:11).

When the children of Israel reached the Red Sea, they might have concluded that God had abandoned His promise to them. The sea was barring their advance, and the murderous Egyptian army was racing to overtake them (see Ex. 14:9-10). Yet God proved then, as He has ever since, that He's absolutely faithful to every word He speaks to His children.

Near the end of his life, Joshua took time with the Israelites to review all God had done for them since they first began following Him. God had given them an impossible assignment: to conquer a foreign, hostile land with fortified cities and armies more powerful than their own. The Israelites were to go forward with nothing more than God's promise that He'd go with them and take care of them. Now Joshua looked back over their experience and reminded the Israelites that God had kept every promise. They had experienced numerous victories and had enjoyed God's provision for every need (see Josh. 24:1-28).

God may have spoken to you about something in particular—a ministry in your church, the way to raise your children, or directions for your job. You've obeyed Him, but now you face a Red Sea experience. It seems what you thought God wanted to accomplish isn't happening. Perhaps your ministry hasn't been well received, your children are rebelling, or coworkers are criticizing your actions.

Trust in the character of God. His nature is to be faithful. Regardless of how bleak your present circumstances are, don't lose hope. No one has ever experienced unfaithfulness on God's part. Allow time for God to reveal His faithfulness to you. Someday you'll reflect on what God has done, and you'll praise Him for His absolute faithfulness to you.

Sometimes hindsight gives us a clear picture of how faithful God has been. We're tempted during a crisis to wonder whether God will be faithful to His promises. We focus on our problems, and our trust in God begins to waver. Twenty-four years after God promised Abraham and Sarah a son, they were still waiting on God to fulfill His promise. But in the 25th year Abraham and Sarah could look back and see that God had been faithful. As David was fleeing for his life, he may have been uncertain about how God would keep His promise to make him a king. But at the end of his long, prosperous reign, David could review ways God had kept every promise.

You too can rely on God's faithfulness. Are you in a crisis? Hold to the promises of your Lord. He won't forget His promises to you. Look back over your Christian life and recount the many ways God has been faithful to His word.

What has God called you to do that will be impossible to accomplish unless God miraculously intervenes?

Take a moment to review God's faithfulness in your past. In hindsight how have you experienced His power, even if you didn't recognize it at the time? How does God's past activity in your life give you confidence for the future?

What biblical story gives you the most encouragement in your current situation? What biblical character do you most relate to? Why?

What was the most meaningful statement or Scripture you read today?

Reword the statement or Scripture into a prayer of response to God.

What does God want you to do in response to today's study?

How Am I Experiencing God?

Use this space to journal about your experience with God,
in particular Reality 5: God's invitation for you to work with Him
always leads you to a crisis of belief that requires faith and action.

GROUP SESSION—REALITY 5
GOD'S INVITATION FOR YOU TO WORK WITH HIM ALWAYS LEADS YOU TO A CRISIS OF BELIEF THAT REQUIRES FAITH AND ACTION

START

Start with review and prayer. Ask volunteers to summarize the truths discussed last week in the study of Exodus 3:1-22.

Ask God to help everyone respond with faith and action to whatever He reveals.

READ & RESPOND

Transition to a study of the biblical text and Reality 5. Read aloud Exodus 4:1-17.

Use the following questions to discuss examples of Reality 5 in Exodus 4:1-17. (Refer to p. 89 for an overview of Reality 5, if needed.)

What tasks did God call Moses to do that were impossible or unexplainable in Moses' own ability (see 4:3-9,11; also recall 3:10-22)?

At what points did Moses clearly express his crisis of belief (see 4:1,10,13; also recall 3:11,13)?

What do Moses' questions reveal about his view of himself? What do his questions reveal about his belief in God's ability, despite the miraculous nature of the whole experience?

What encouragement do you receive in seeing that even so-called heroes of the faith wrestled with a crisis of belief?

How did God overcome Moses' objections, moving Moses to faith and action (see 4:3-9,11,14-17)?

What's revealed about God's character in the simple fact that He responded to Moses' concerns?

What other examples in Scripture can you recall when God invited people to do things that were humanly impossible?

REVIEW

Continue the discussion on a personal level by connecting themes from the daily reading with Reality 5. (Allow these questions to serve as a guide, but feel free to discuss any meaningful statements from or actions taken in response to the daily reading.)

Day 1

With what decision are you currently wrestling? Why?

What do your hesitations and excuses reveal about your belief in God?

Day 2

In what areas of your life have you been overcomplicating God's will or feeling confused about what He wants you to do?

Day 3

Don't hide your doubts or questions. Give them to Jesus. How do you struggle to believe in God, God's goodness, or God's power?

Day 4

In what specific ways have you been comparing your circumstances (or abilities, like Moses' speech) to other people's lives (or abilities)?

How does the promise that God's love for you is greater than even the most difficult circumstances (see Rom. 8:35-39) give you hope and confidence?

Day 5

What has God called you to do that will be impossible to accomplish unless God miraculously intervenes?

Take a moment to review God's faithfulness in your past. In hindsight how have you experienced His power, even if you didn't recognize it at the time? How does God's past activity in your life give you confidence for the future?

EXPERIENCING GOD STORIES

Use this opportunity to share ways you've experienced God.

How have you experienced God this past week?

When have you experienced a crisis of belief, and how did you respond with faith and action?

WRAP UP

Conclude the session by reading this final thought and then closing in prayer.

God's assignments have God-sized dimensions. If what you believe about God doesn't stretch you out of your comfort zone, it probably isn't God. Let Him use you in ways you never would have asked, dreamed, or imagined.

Next week we'll discuss Reality 6: You must make major adjustments in your life to join God in what He is doing.

REALITY 6
ADJUST

You must make major adjustments in your life
to join God in what He is doing.

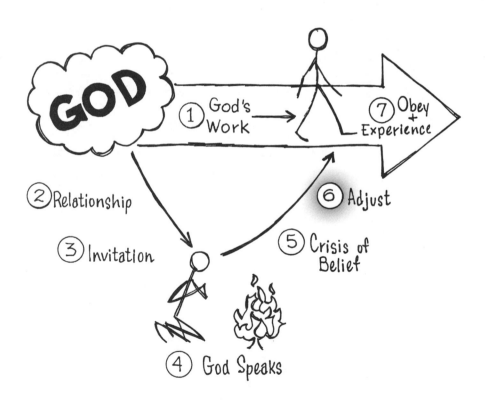

Like the crisis of belief, the necessity of adjustment is a second point at which many people miss out on experiencing God. To get from where you are to where God is requires significant adjustments in your life. These adjustments may relate to your thinking, circumstances, relationships, commitments, actions, and beliefs. To move from your way of thinking or acting to God's way of thinking or acting always requires fundamental adjustments. You can't stay where you are and go with God at the same time.

Moses had to make major changes in his life to join God in what He was doing. Moses couldn't stay in the desert and stand before Pharaoh at the same time. God said, " 'Go back to Egypt, for all those who wanted to kill you are dead.' So Moses took his wife and sons, put them on a donkey and started back to Egypt" (Ex. 4:19-20).

For Moses to make the required adjustments to orient his life to God, he had to become convinced that God could do everything He said He'd do. Then Moses had to leave his job and extended family and move to Egypt. When he fled Egypt 40 years earlier, he'd been a fugitive. Returning to the court of Pharaoh could have been tantamount to turning himself over to the authorities who wanted to punish him severely. Moses had to believe God could do what He said, or else Moses' life was in grave danger.

After determining to move forward, Moses was in a position to obey God. That didn't mean he was going to do something all by himself for God. It meant he was going to be where God was working. Then God would do what He'd purposed through Moses. Moses was a servant who was moldable, and he remained at God's disposal to be used as God chose. God accomplished His extraordinary purposes through the ordinary shepherd Moses.

GO!

Go and make disciples of all nations, baptizing them in the
name of the Father and of the Son and of the Holy Spirit.
MATTHEW 28:19

Our Master commands us to go. We need to get His permission to stay! The gospel is the account of Jesus' leaving His Father's right hand to go to Calvary. Jesus instructed those who wanted to be His disciples to leave their homes and their comforts and follow Him (see Luke 9:57-58). Some insisted they couldn't go yet because they still had to care for elderly parents (see vv. 59-60). Others wanted to make sure everything was in order first (see vv. 61-62). Jesus never excused people who struggled to follow Him. He made it clear that to follow Him meant He set the direction and they were to follow.

We can convince ourselves that Jesus doesn't really want us to adjust our lives, pointing to the success we're enjoying where we are. Yet Jesus often told His disciples to go elsewhere in spite of the success they were experiencing. Peter had just pulled in the greatest catch of fish of his entire career when Jesus invited him to leave everything (see Luke 5:1-11). Philip was enjoying astounding success as an evangelist when the Holy Spirit instructed him to go to the desert (see Acts 8:25-26). Success where we are can be our greatest hindrance to going where Jesus wants us to be.

On the other hand, adjusting our lives to God's work may not immediately lead to what looks like success. Moses experienced this truth as he learned how God was going to deliver the Hebrews from Egypt. God told him He'd harden Pharaoh's heart. Yet the result wasn't what Moses anticipated. Rather than allowing the Hebrews to leave, Pharaoh increased their hardship. Rather than becoming a hero among the Hebrews, Moses was despised for bringing greater suffering to them. Moses went to the Lord and asked, "Why, Lord, why have you brought trouble on this people? Is this why you sent me?" (Ex. 5:22). Much of the frustration we experience as Christians has nothing to do with what God does or doesn't do. Rather, it has everything to do with the false assumptions we make about how we think God will and should act.

Have you ever done the will of God, and then things seemed to become worse? Moses completely misunderstood what the results of His obedience to God would be. When things didn't turn out as he anticipated, Moses became discouraged. God had told Moses what to do, but He hadn't told Moses what the consequences would be. It's foolish to attempt to do God's work using your own common sense. God doesn't eliminate your common sense; He consecrates it. He gives you His wisdom so that you can understand His ways.

As you look back on God's activity in your life, you'll recognize the supreme wisdom in the way He has led you. As you look forward to what God may do, be careful not to become too comfortable where you are or to predict what He has for you next. If you do, you may resist Christ's invitation to go elsewhere. He may lead you across the street to share the gospel with your neighbor or to the other side of the world. Wherever He leads, be prepared to go.

What success or comfort could tempt you to resist Christ's invitation to go do something else? What apparent failure is discouraging you from trusting God's call to join His work?

How will you adjust your expectations and your willingness to be used by God whenever, however, and wherever He chooses?

What was the most meaningful statement or Scripture you read today?

Reword the statement or Scripture into a prayer of response to God.

What does God want you to do in response to today's study?

day 2
GOD'S INITIATIVE

*Now to him who is able to do immeasurably
more than all we ask or imagine, according to
his power that is at work within us ...*
EPHESIANS 3:20

At times we feel as if we could impress God with all we're trying to do for Him and His church. Yet God isn't impressed with even the most grandiose human aspirations (see Ps. 8:3-4). You'll never set a goal so big or attempt a task so significant that God doesn't have something far greater that He could do in and through your life. Saul of Tarsus worked harder than anyone else to impress God with his efforts, only to discover that his greatest achievements were just garbage compared to God's will for his life (see Phil. 3:7-8).

Our problem is that we become too easily enamored with our own plans. If we're attempting to do noble or difficult things, we assume that we must be experiencing the maximum potential for our lives and that God, therefore, must be pleased with us. But until we've heard from God, we can't even imagine all our lives could become or all God could accomplish through us.

The most dramatic changes in your life will come from God's initiative, not yours. The people God used mightily in Scripture were all ordinary people to whom He gave divine assignments they never could have initiated. The Lord often took them by surprise, for they weren't seeking significant mandates from God. Even so, He saw their hearts, and He knew they were trustworthy.

The Lord spoke to Abram when He was beginning to build a nation dedicated to His purposes. Through this nation would come the Savior. God appeared to Moses at the very time He had purposed to deliver Israel from slavery in Egypt. God found in Jesse's youngest son, David, a godly man who could lead His people. God surprised Mary when He told her she'd be the mother of the Messiah. God's Son selected the twelve disciples—all ordinary, uneducated men—when He was ready to take the good news of His salvation to the world. Through the ages God has taken the initiative in the everyday lives of people to accomplish things through them that they never could have imagined.

The Lord may be initiating some new things in your life. When He tells you what His plans are, trust Him and walk closely with Him. Don't let the busyness of your present activity keep you from experiencing all God has in store for you. You'll see Him accomplish things through your life that you never dreamed possible (see Eph. 3:20).

We need to remind ourselves that the Father sees the big picture, that His power far exceeds our limited imagination. We must set aside our own agenda, no matter how lofty. We must never become satisfied with our own dreams, for they are finite at best. When we follow God's direction, we'll witness things happening in our lives that can be explained only by His powerful presence. How could we be satisfied with anything less?

What plans of your own do you honestly feel should impress God or deserve His blessing?

What area of your life would be the easiest to adjust to God's will? What area would be the most difficult or significant to adjust if God required change?

What will you do to completely open yourself up to God's initiative?

What was the most meaningful statement or Scripture you read today?

Reword the statement or Scripture into a prayer of response to God.

What does God want you to do in response to today's study?

day 3
A LIVING SACRIFICE

I urge you, brothers and sisters, in view of God's mercy,
to offer your bodies as a living sacrifice, holy and pleasing
to God—this is your true and proper worship.
ROMANS 12:1

God takes great pleasure in worthy sacrifices. In the Old Testament He gave detailed instructions for the way His people were to give their offerings, declaring that these brought "an aroma pleasing" to Him (Lev. 1:13,17). When the Israelites gave an offering to God, it was no longer their own; it belonged entirely to God. God would accept only the best that people could give. Offering animals that were damaged or imperfect in any way was an affront to Almighty God.

A worthy sacrifice had to cost the people something. As their hearts shifted away from God, the people began struggling with the command to give God costly offerings. Instead, they brought blind, lame, and sick animals, assuming God couldn't tell the difference (see Mal. 1:8). God saw what they were doing and declared their offerings to be in vain (v. 10).

Throughout the Old Testament period God was setting the stage for the ultimate, perfect, and sinless sacrifice of His Son for the sins of humanity. God Himself met the standard for sacrifices when He offered His own Son as the spotless Lamb. Only the death of His perfect Son was an offering worthy enough to atone for the sins of humankind. God's love moved Him to sacrifice what meant the most to Him—His only Son.

Our response, if we truly understand His love for us, is the desire to give back to God what means the most to us. Now God asks us to lay down our lives on His altar as living sacrifices (see Rom. 12:1). Just as in the Old Testament, our sacrifice, once offered, can't be reclaimed. We belong entirely to God. We can't make a partial sacrifice of our lives; our offering must be wholehearted.

Therefore, if you're a Christian, your life isn't your own. Rather than dying, however, God asks you to live for Him as a living sacrifice. Every day you're to offer your life to Him for His service. You don't serve Him in your spare time or with your leftover resources. The way you live your life for God is your offering to Him. Relentlessly pursue holiness so that your offering to God is unblemished and acceptable to Him (see Eph. 4:1; Phil. 1:27; 1 Thess. 2:12).

The offerings we give to God reveal the condition of our heart. A heart that overflows with gratitude for God's love responds in selfless devotion. If we're unwilling to sacrifice our time, our possessions, our money, or our energy, we indicate that we don't fully love God. God takes delight in someone who cheerfully gives to Him from a loving heart, someone who understands that God is the source of everything he has and who knows God will more than compensate for whatever is sacrificed for Him (see 2 Cor. 9:8). If you struggle in giving your best offerings to God, pause and reflect on what God sacrificed for you. Trust Him and give Him the best you have because you love Him with all your heart.

What's been the most significant sacrifice in your life? How did God prove more satisfying than whatever you sacrificed?

Based on your life experiences and in your own words, what does it mean to be a living sacrifice in general? What specific adjustments do you need to make to live in wholehearted gratitude for Jesus' ultimate sacrifice?

What do you value most? How can you completely trust Jesus with that?

What was the most meaningful statement or Scripture you read today?

Reword the statement or Scripture into a prayer of response to God.

What does God want you to do in response to today's study?

day 4
MAKING ROOM FOR GOD'S WORK

Enlarge the place of your tent,
stretch your tent curtains wide,
do not hold back;
lengthen your cords,
strengthen your stakes.
ISAIAH 54:2

When Almighty God encounters a life, it's always a time of rejoicing and expectation for the future. Isaiah described this experience as similar to that of a child born to a previously barren woman. The child's arrival changes everything. Whereas the dwelling place might have been large enough for two, it must now be made bigger. The child's presence causes the parents to completely rearrange the way they've been living.

Isaiah proclaimed that when God comes, you must make room for Him in your life. You must "enlarge the place of your tent" because God's presence will add new dimensions to your life, your family, and your church. You don't simply add Christ to your busy life and carry on with business as usual. When Christ is your Lord, everything changes. Whereas before you may not have expected good things to come through you or into your life, now you should have a spirit of optimism. You ought to expect your life to become richer and fuller. You can anticipate God blessing others through your life. You can look for God to demonstrate His power through your life in increasing measure.

God rewards people who are faithful to Him. Throughout your life God seeks to grow your faith. He continually brings you to times when you must trust Him. He leads you into situations that require a little faith, and if you're faithful, He will then take you into situations that require even greater trust in Him. Each time you're able to trust God at a higher level, He will reveal more of Himself to you. Your faith and experiencing God are directly linked.

The best way to determine whether you're prepared for a greater revelation of God is to evaluate how faithful you've been with what God has already given you. This is a foundational principle in God's relationships with us: if you've been faithful with the little He's given you, you're ready to be entrusted with more (see Luke 16:10). If you failed to trust God with the little He gave you, He won't trust you with more. God won't lead you beyond your present level of trust and obedience to Him. He will return you to your area of unfaithfulness until you're prepared to trust Him. The children of Israel were unwilling to trust God to lead them into the promised land, and tragically, their generation was never again able to move forward with Him.

As a Christian, how do you make room for Christ in your life? You repent of your sin. You allow Christ the freedom to do what He wants in you. You eagerly watch for His activity. You live your life with the expectancy that Christ will fill you with His power in the days to come and will stretch you to do things in His service that you've never done before.

How has God's presence changed your life?

Consider the steps of faith you've taken in the past. In what ways have you trusted God and proved faithful with the little things?

How are you making room for God to do greater things in and through your life?

What was the most meaningful statement or Scripture you read today?

Reword the statement or Scripture into a prayer of response to God.

What does God want you to do in response to today's study?

day 5
NOBODY CAN STOP YOU

The LORD said to Joshua, "Do not be afraid
of them; I have given them into your hand.
Not one of them will be able to withstand you."
JOSHUA 10:8

Have you ever felt that someone was thwarting God's will for you? Perhaps someone kept you from getting a job or earning a promotion. Perhaps the government wouldn't approve your application, or a committee disagreed with your recommendation. Do you believe mere human beings can stop God from accomplishing His purposes in your life?

The decisions and disobedience of others can't cancel God's will for you. Other people's actions affect you, but no one can prevent what God wants to do in and through you. Joshua and Caleb trusted God and yet were forced to wander in a wilderness for 40 years because of the fear and disbelief of others.

God did everything He intended to do in the lives of Joshua and Caleb. His primary assignment for them hadn't been to enter the promised land but rather to serve as godly leaders for their people. Joshua and Caleb couldn't lead the people if they entered the promised land by themselves while the people were still wandering in the wilderness. God kept these leaders in a position where they could exert a godly influence on their nation, and as a result, they became models of spiritual leadership for generations to come. Even so, God ultimately brought Caleb and Joshua into the promised land just as He'd said. They'd been delayed but not thwarted. Be assured of this: no one can hinder God from carrying out His plans for your life. Once God sets something in motion, no one can stop it (see Isa. 46:11).

No greater confidence will ever come to you or to any other Christian than the assurance of knowing you're doing God's will. He won't commission you to do anything without ensuring your success. God assured Joshua that there was no reason to fear as he prepared to battle the Canaanites. God would allow the Israelites to fight the battle, but the outcome was settled before they ever picked up their weapons. What confidence this gave them as they fought! Even though their enemies fought relentlessly, Joshua's army was certain of eventual victory. God doesn't promise you victory in every task you devise, but He does promise that you'll be successful whenever you follow His will (see Deut. 28:7).

Does it appear that people are keeping you from obeying God's will? Rest assured that God won't allow anyone or anything to prevent His children from accomplishing His purposes. Be careful to evaluate success the way God does.

When it appears that you're being thwarted in doing God's will, perhaps He's working to produce His peace in your heart as you face troubling times. Perhaps He's working to develop a forgiving spirit in you when others mistreat you. Perhaps He's working to eliminate a particular sin in your life. If you accept the world's understanding of victory, you may feel defeated. But if you look to see what God's accomplishing through your situation, you'll find that He's succeeding. When you face opposition but know you're doing what God has asked, have confidence that He will accomplish everything He desires.

What have you felt has been getting in the way of God's will in your life? How have you blamed other people or circumstances for the spiritual condition of your life?

How can you join God's work right where you are, even if your circumstance feels like a detour or a delay in a bigger plan?

What failure have you experienced? How does that failure redirect you to God's will?

What was the most meaningful statement or Scripture you read today?

Reword the statement or Scripture into a prayer of response to God.

What does God want you to do in response to today's study?

How Am I Experiencing God?

Use this space to journal about your experience with God,
in particular Reality 6: You must make major adjustments
in your life to join God in what He is doing.

GROUP SESSION—REALITY 6
YOU MUST MAKE MAJOR ADJUSTMENTS IN YOUR LIFE TO JOIN GOD IN WHAT HE IS DOING

START

Start with review and prayer. Ask volunteers to summarize the truths discussed last week in the study of Exodus 4:1-17.

Ask God to give people the courage to make major adjustments in their lives to join God in what He is doing. Pray that everyone will be dissatisfied and uncomfortable until they align their lives with the mainstream of God's activity.

READ & RESPOND

Transition to a study of the biblical text and Reality 6. Read aloud Exodus 4:18–5:9.

Use the following questions to discuss examples of Reality 6 in Exodus 4:18–5:9. (Refer to p. 107 for an overview of Reality 6, if needed.)

What major adjustments were neccesary for Moses to join God's work (see 4:18-20,24-26)?

How does the mention of Egyptians who had wanted Moses dead add to your understanding of Moses' crisis of belief and his major adjustment to join God in what He was doing (see 4:19)?

What does the story about circumcision, the sign of God's covenant with the Israelites, suggest about Moses' previous relationship with God and the community of God's people (see 4:24-26)? How does it highlight the major adjustments required of Moses and people around Him?

Making major adjustments isn't easy and doesn't guarantee immediate success. How did the following people respond to the major adjustments in Moses' life?

☐ Jethro, his father-in-law (see 4:18)
☐ Zipporah, his wife (see 4:25)
☐ Aaron, his brother (see 4:27-29)
☐ Elders and Israelites (see 4:31)
☐ Pharaoh (see 5:2-9)

REVIEW
Continue the discussion on a personal level by connecting themes from the daily reading with Reality 6. (Allow these questions to serve as a guide, but feel free to discuss any meaningful statements from or actions taken in response to the daily reading.)

Day 1

What success or comfort could tempt you to resist Christ's invitation to go do something else? What apparent failure is discouraging you from trusting God's call to join His work?

How will you adjust your expectations and your willingness to be used by God whenever, however, and wherever He chooses?

Day 2

What area of your life would be the easiest to adjust to God's will?
What area would be the most difficult or significant to adjust if
God required change?

What will you do to completely open yourself up to God's initiative?

Day 3

What's been the most significant sacrifice in your life? How did God prove
more satisfying than whatever you sacrificed?

Based on your life experiences and in your own words, what does it mean
to be a living sacrifice in general? What specific adjustments do you need
to make to live in wholehearted gratitude for Jesus' ultimate sacrifice?

Day 4

How has God's presence changed your life?

Consider the steps of faith you've taken in the past. In what ways have
you trusted God and proved faithful with the little things?

Day 5

What have you felt has been getting in the way of God's will in your life?
How have you blamed other people or circumstances for the spiritual
condition of your life?

EXPERIENCING GOD STORIES

Use this opportunity to share ways you've experienced God.

How have you experienced God this past week?

What major adjustments have you made to join God in what He is doing, and how have you experienced Him as a result?

WRAP UP

Conclude your time by reading this final thought and then closing in prayer.

You can't stay where you are and go with God
at the same time. If you truly want to know and
do the will of God, do whatever it takes today
to get into the mainstream of His activity.

Next week we'll discuss Reality 7: You come
to know God by experience as you obey Him,
and He accomplishes His work through you.

REALITY 7
OBEY & EXPERIENCE

You come to know God by experience as you obey Him,
and He accomplishes His work through you.

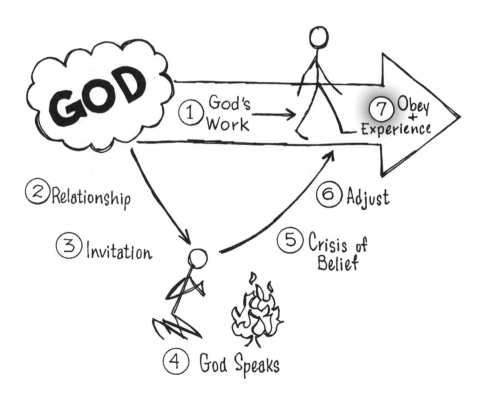

Once you've determined to follow God by faith and you've made the necessary adjustments, you must obey Him. When you do what God tells you, no matter how impossible or bewildering it may seem, He carries out what He purposed through you. Not only do you experience God's power and presence, but so do those who observe your life.

Moses came to know God by experience as he obeyed God, and God accomplished His work through him. Many Scripture passages illustrate how God spoke to Moses and brought him into a deeper understanding of who He is. As Moses obeyed God, God accomplished through him what Moses couldn't do on his own. Moses must have felt humbled and unworthy to be used in such significant ways. Yet Moses obeyed and did everything God told him. Then God accomplished through Moses all He intended. Every step of obedience brought Moses (and Israel) to a greater knowledge of God (see Ex. 6:1-8).

Even today God is reconciling a world to Himself. Because He loves you, He wants to involve you in His activity. He begins by pursuing a love relationship with you. He then invites you to become involved with Him in His work. As He relates to you, He discloses Himself, His purposes, and His ways. If you want to experience God's mighty power at work in and through you, you must walk by faith, make major adjustments, and obey whatever God tells you to do.

day 1
KNOWING GOD MORE

God also said to Moses, "I am the Lord. I appeared to
Abraham, to Isaac and to Jacob as God Almighty, but by my
name the Lord I did not make myself fully known to them."
EXODUS 6:2-3

When Moses encountered God in the burning bush, he still had much to learn about his Lord. Moses was impressed with the miracle before him (see Ex. 3:3). However, it would take much more than a burning bush to lead Israel out of captivity by the most powerful nation of Moses' day. Would the same God who could cause a bush to burn without being consumed also be able to do what was necessary to deliver a multitude? Moses had much more to learn through experience and still had many questions.

God's answer was "I AM" (v. 14). That is, "Moses, I'll be whatever you need Me to be as you carry out My assignment. If you need miraculous signs in order to convince Pharaoh, then that's how I'll express Myself. If you need Me to interrupt nature and part the waters of the Red Sea, then I'll demonstrate Myself that way. If you require food and water, then I'll be your provider. If you're afraid, I'll be your strength."

At the beginning of Moses' walk with the Lord, he had no way of knowing everything he'd need God to do for him. Yet each time Moses faced a need, He learned something new about God. Moses came to realize that there was much more to God than a burning bush. What if Moses had been so enamored with his experience at the bush that he built a tabernacle on the spot and established The Church of the Burning Bush? He would have missed out on so much more that God wanted to reveal to him.

As God has walked with His people through the generations, He's progressively revealed His nature according to His purposes and the needs of His people. Abraham, Isaac, and Jacob knew Him as God Almighty because they needed His mighty power to protect them from their enemies. Moses and the Israelites learned that God was Lord, the Master over every nation and every enemy army. God not only delivered them from the most powerful ruler in the world but also brought them into the promised land. They came to experience Him as Lord, preeminently powerful over the pagan gods of their day.

God will continue to reveal His character to you according to your needs and according to His purposes. You'll come to know more and more about Him as you obey Him. When you grieve, He will come to you as Comforter. When you're in need, He will demonstrate that He's the Provider. When you face a serious challenge, He will reveal that He's God Almighty.

Your understanding of God's character ought to be greater now than when you first became a Christian. You ought to know Him better today than you did five years ago. Sadly, some Christians continue to live year after year with the same basic knowledge of God they had when they first began walking with Him. Whatever your present situation, view it in light of what God is teaching you about Himself, and you'll come to know God in dimensions you've never known before.

You stand at an exciting new door of opportunity to know God more intimately every time you believe Him. Every step of faith leads you to a deeper relationship of faith with Him. It's an open invitation to know God more intimately.

Recall your understanding of God when you first began walking with Him. How have your experiences expanded your knowledge of Him?

How does Moses' story help you better understand your own relationship with God?

What was the most meaningful statement or Scripture you read today?

Reword the statement or Scripture into a prayer of response to God.

What does God want you to do in response to today's study?

day 2
FAITHFUL AT EVERY STEP

God said, "Take your son, your only son, whom you love—
Isaac—and go to the region of Moriah. Sacrifice him there
as a burnt offering on a mountain I will show you."
GENESIS 22:2

Our difficulty in following God isn't that we don't know His will. Our discomfort comes from the fact that we *do* know His will, but we don't want to do it. When God first spoke to Abraham, His commands were straightforward: "Go ... to the land I will show you" (Gen. 12:1). Then God led Abraham through a number of tests over the years. Abraham learned patience as he waited for God's promise of a son to be fulfilled, which took 25 years. Abraham learned to trust God through battles with kings and through the destruction of Sodom and Gomorrah.

The pinnacle of Abraham's walk of faith was when God asked him to sacrifice the one thing that meant more to him than anything else. Abraham's previous obedience indicated that he would have quickly and decisively sacrificed anything else God asked of him, but was he prepared for this? God didn't ask Abraham to make such a significant sacrifice at the beginning of their relationship. Rather, it came more than 30 years after Abraham began walking with God. God taught Abraham to trust Him step-by-step.

As the Father progressively reveals His ways to you in your Christian pilgrimage, you, like Abraham, will develop a deeper level of trust in Him. When you first became a Christian, your Master's instructions were probably fundamental, such as being baptized or changing your lifestyle. But as you learn to trust Him more deeply, He will develop your character to match bigger tests, and with the greater tests will come a greater love for God and a greater knowledge of His ways. Are you ready for God's next revelation?

As God leads you in your Christian growth, He will allow challenges in your life that match your character and relationship with Him. God won't totally change your character at once when you become a Christian. Rather, He will lead you through a process to become more like His Son. He will keep working in an area of your life until it's controlled by the Holy Spirit. You may eagerly desire maturity in every area of your character, but steady, gradual growth is more lasting.

God won't take shortcuts in His process of making you like Christ. Because He sees your life from eternity, He will take as long as necessary to produce lasting spiritual growth in you.

Don't become impatient while God is producing Christlikeness in you. Don't seek more responsibilities than those He's given you. Obey all you know He's asked, and He will lead you at a pace that fits your present character and His purposes for you.

What aspect of God's will are you currently struggling with? Why is this step of faith hard for you?

What's been the scariest step of faith so far in your walk with God? What made it so significant? How did God prove faithful?

How has your character been conformed more to the likeness of Jesus through steps of obedience? What qualities of your character are clearly the result of God's work in you?

What was the most meaningful statement or Scripture you read today?

Reword the statement or Scripture into a prayer of response to God.

What does God want you to do in response to today's study?

day 3
TAKING GOD
AT HIS WORD

He sent two of his disciples,
telling them, "Go into the city."
MARK 14:13

Two disciples were given very detailed instructions to go to a certain town and look for a particular man performing a specific task. He'd have a large room, furnished and ready to observe the Passover. These instructions might have seemed unusual had it not been their Lord speaking, but the two disciples obeyed and found everything just as Jesus had said. Jesus knew exactly what they'd find, so He guided them specifically. One of the most memorable and precious times the disciples would spend with their Teacher hinged on the obedience of these two.

Obedience to Christ's commands always brings fulfillment. His word is His promise. When the Lord gives you instructions, obey immediately. Don't wait until you've figured it all out and everything makes perfect sense to you. Sometimes God leads you to do things you won't fully understand until you've done them. He doesn't usually reveal all the details of His will when He first speaks to you. Instead, He tells you enough for you to implement what He's said, but He withholds enough information so that you must continue to rely on His guidance.

Your response to God will affect what He does next in your life. Your obedience may affect the way others around you experience Christ as well. If God's given you a directive you haven't obeyed, immediately obey that word and watch God's perfect plan unfold in your life. You'll experience His faithfulness as He fulfills His promises.

When we walk in intimate fellowship with Christ, we have the assurance that every promise God has made in Scripture is available to us. This truth should motivate us to search the Scriptures for each promise in order to meditate on its potential for our lives.

Jesus promised that when you ask for something in His will, He will give you what you ask (see John 16:23b). This promise is available to every Christian. If you ask God whether this promise applies to your life, His answer is yes. If you aren't currently experiencing this promise, it doesn't change the fact that God has said it. You may need to seek God's answer for why His promise hasn't yet reached maturity in you.

Paul claimed he'd tested each of these promises in his life and found them all to be abundantly true. That's why he could speak of "the incomparable riches of his grace, expressed in his kindness to us in Christ Jesus" (Eph. 2:7) and "the boundless riches of Christ" (3:8). Paul had found a wealth of God's promises and enjoyed them all in abundance.

Don't become discouraged or impatient if you aren't experiencing to the fullest all God's promises in your life. God may want to prepare you to receive some of the great truths He's made available to you. Walk closely with your Lord, and in time you'll see Him bring His promises to fruition in your life.

What promise in Scripture has been most significant in your past? Why?

What promise in Scripture gives you confidence for the future? Why?

On a scale of 1 to 10 (1 = stubborn rebellion; 10 = eager obedience), how obedient are you to God's Word?

What was the most meaningful statement or Scripture you read today?

Reword the statement or Scripture into a prayer of response to God.

What does God want you to do in response to today's study?

day 4
OBEDIENCE IS LOVE

Whoever has my commands and keeps them is the one who loves me. The one who loves me will be loved by my Father, and I too will love them and show myself to them.

JOHN 14:21

Obedience to God's commands comes from your heart. When you begin struggling to obey God, that's a clear indication that your heart has shifted away from Him. Some claim, "I love God, but I'm having difficulty obeying Him in certain areas of my life." That's a spiritual impossibility. If I asked you, "Do you love God?" you might easily respond, "Yes." However, if I asked you, "Are you obeying God?" would you answer yes as quickly? Yet I'd be asking you the same question!

Genuine love for God leads to wholehearted obedience. If you told your spouse that you loved her at certain times but that you struggled to love her at others, your relationship would be in jeopardy. Yet we assume God's satisfied with occasional love or partial obedience. He isn't.

Obedience without love is legalism. Obedience for its own sake can be nothing more than perfectionism, which leads to pride. Many conscientious Christians seek to cultivate discipline in their lives to be more obedient to Christ. As helpful as spiritual disciplines can be, they can never replace your love for God. Love is the discipline. God looks beyond your godly habits, beyond your moral lifestyle, and beyond your church involvement and focuses His penetrating gaze on your heart.

Has your worship become empty and routine? Have you lost your motivation to read God's Word? Has your prayer life been reduced to a ritual? These are symptoms of a heart that's shifted away from God. You can't be close to God without being affected by His love. Love is the greatest motivation for a relationship with God and for serving Him.

The Heavenly Father loved His Son with an eternal love. Everything in the Father's heart and life was released to His Son. As the Father expressed His love for a broken and sinful world, this passion was manifested through the life of His Son. The Father initiated His plan to save humankind, and from a heart of devotion the Son accepted the assignment that took Him to the cross.

As Jesus walked among people, the Father's love filled His Son. Jesus recognized that no ordinary love could motivate Him to go to the cross. No human love could keep Him perfectly obedient to His Father throughout His life. Only His Father's love was powerful enough to compel Him to commit His life to the saving purpose of His Father.

Jesus prayed that God would place this same love in His disciples (see John 17:26). He knew no other motivation would be sufficient for the assignments God had for them. God's answer was to place His Son in them. It's impossible for a Christian to be filled with this measure of love and not to be on mission with God.

You'll be incapable of ministering to everyone God sends to you unless you have His love. You can't forgive others, go the extra mile with others, or sacrifice for others unless you've first been filled with the boundless love of God. Seek to know the Father and His immeasurable love; then allow His Son to love others through you.

What does your current obedience reveal about your love for and relationship with God? (Review your response to yesterday's scale.)

How does God's love for you affect your thoughts, decisions, and behavior? How does your love for God influence your thoughts, decisions, and behavior?

What was the most meaningful statement or Scripture you read today?

Reword the statement or Scripture into a prayer of response to God.

What does God want you to do in response to today's study?

day 5

POWER IN PERSEVERANCE

*As the time approached for him to be taken up
to heaven, Jesus resolutely set out for Jerusalem.*
LUKE 9:51

It's easy to become distracted or discouraged in the Christian life. The moment you understand what God wants you to do, it will seem as though everyone around you requires your time and attention.

When the time came for Jesus to go to the cross, He "resolutely set out for Jerusalem" so that nothing would prevent Him from accomplishing His Father's will. So obvious was His resolve to go to Jerusalem that the Samaritans, who hated the Jews, rejected Him because they recognized that He was a Jew traveling through their village to the hated city of Jerusalem (see Luke 9:52-53).

Jesus determined not to digress from His mission, but He took time to minister to many people along His way. He sent out 72 disciples into the surrounding towns (see 10:1). He healed lepers (see 17:11-19). He cured a man of dropsy (see 14:1-4). He brought salvation to the home of Zacchaeus (see 19:1-10). He continued to teach His disciples (see 15). Jesus didn't refuse to minister to others as He went to Calvary, but ultimately, He refused to be deterred from His Father's will.

If you know what God wants you to do, resolutely set your sights toward that goal with full determination to accomplish it (see Prov. 4:25). Beware of becoming so sidetracked by the opportunities around you that you lose sight of God's ultimate goal for you. Don't succumb to the temptation to delay your obedience or to discard it altogether. Once you've received a clear assignment from God, your response should be unwavering focus and obedience.

What you choose to focus on becomes the dominant influence in your life. You may be a Christian, but if your focus is always on your problems, your problems will determine the direction of your life. If your focus is on people, then people will determine what you think and do. When you choose to focus on Christ, you naturally move closer to Him. You experience His power.

Christ is at your right hand (see Ps. 16:8). In biblical times the right hand was the most distinguished position, reserved for someone's chief adviser and supporter. Every time you face a new experience, you should turn to Christ for His strength. When people insult you and mistreat you, you should seek direction from your Counselor about the right response. When you face a crisis, you should receive strength from the One at your right hand. When you experience need, you should consult your Counselor before you react. When you face a fearful situation, you should take courage from the Advocate at your right hand. Everything you do is in the context of your relationship with Christ.

What an incredible act of God's grace that Christ stands beside you to guide you, counsel you, and defend you! How could you ever become dismayed over your situation with Christ at your right hand? What confidence this should give you! Don't give up. Stay focused on Christ. Determine to follow Him.

In what areas of your walk with Jesus are you tired, discouraged, or distracted?

What do you know God wants you to do?

How will you persevere toward that goal? What practical steps will you take to continually rely on the Lord's power and wisdom?

What was the most meaningful statement or Scripture you read today?

Reword the statement or Scripture into a prayer of response to God.

What does God want you to do in response to today's study?

How Am I Experiencing God?

Use this space to journal about your experience with God,
in particular Reality 7: You come to know God by experience
as you obey Him, and He accomplishes His work through you.

GROUP SESSION—REALITY 7
YOU COME TO KNOW GOD BY EXPERIENCE AS YOU OBEY HIM, AND HE ACCOMPLISHES HIS WORK THROUGH YOU

START

Start with review and prayer. Ask volunteers to summarize the truths discussed last week in the study of Exodus 4:18–5:9.

Ask God to change each person's life forever as they come to know God by experience through obedience. Thank God for the work He will accomplish in and through each individual and this group.

READ & RESPOND

Transition to a study of the biblical text and Reality 7. Use the following questions to discuss examples of Reality 7 in each passage. (Refer to p. 125 for an overview of Reality 7, if needed.)

Read aloud Exodus 5:22–6:9.

What examples of the previous six realities for experiencing God do you see in this passage?

1. God's work (see 6:1-5)
2. Relationship (see 6:2-8)
3. Invitation (see 6:6)
4. God speaks (see 6:1-2,8)
5. Crisis of belief (see 5:22-23; 6:9)
6. Adjust (see 6:9)

What did God promise to accomplish? What would His people experience through Moses' obedience?

How did God keep this promise? Briefly summarize what you know about the plagues and Israel's escape through the Red Sea (see Ex. 7–14).

Following God's display of power over Egypt through the plagues and the exodus, He continued to miraculously provide for His people and began forming them into a nation under His sovereign authority, despite their continual grumbling and lack of trust in Him. He provided the law, including the Ten Commandments, and instructions for worship, including the tabernacle, through His servant, Moses.

Read aloud Exodus 33:1–34:10,27-35.

How did Moses come to know God by experience (see 33:7-11,14,17-23; 34:5-8,29)?

What work did God accomplish through Moses (see 33:1; 34:28)?

How did other people also come to know God by experience through Moses' obedience (see 33:1; 34:8-10,30-35)?

REVIEW

Continue the discussion on a personal level by connecting themes from the daily reading with Reality 7. (Allow these questions to serve as a guide, but feel free to discuss any meaningful statements from or actions taken in response to the daily reading.)

Day 1

Recall your understanding of God when you first began walking with Him. How have your experiences expanded your knowledge of Him?

How does Moses' story help you better understand your own relationship with God?

Day 2

What aspect of God's will are you currently struggling with? Why is this step of faith hard for you?

What's been the scariest step of faith so far in your walk with God? What made it so significant? How did God prove faithful?

Day 3

What promise in Scripture has been most significant in your past? Why?

What promise in Scripture gives you confidence for the future? Why?

On a scale of 1 to 10 (1 = stubborn rebellion; 10 = eager obedience), how obedient are you to God's Word?

Day 4

What does your current obedience reveal about your love for and relationship with God?

Day 5

Moses made time to be in God's presence. He needed God. Nothing he'd experienced was done in his own ability. Moses had nothing to live for or to offer the community around him without the power and wisdom of God. This dependence on God's presence changed Moses in a way that was noticeable to everyone around him. What practical steps will you take to continually rely on the Lord's power and wisdom?

EXPERIENCING GOD STORIES

Use this opportunity to share ways you've experienced God.

How have you experienced God this past week?

With whom do you desire to share your knowledge and experience with God? Like Moses pleading with the Lord for the sake of Israel, to whom will you ask God to show His mercy and make His presence known as He works through you?

WRAP UP

Conclude the study by reading this final thought and then closing in prayer.

When you do what God tells you, no matter how impossible or bewildering it may seem, He carries out what He purposed through you. Not only do you experience God's power and presence, but so do those who observe your life.

Every day is a new opportunity to experience God by joining His work in the world around you.

How to Begin a Personal Relationship with God

The essence of eternal life—and the heart of this study—is for you to personally know God the Father and Jesus Christ, His Son. Knowing God doesn't come through a program, a study, or a method. It's the result of a vibrant, growing, one-on-one relationship with God.

Perhaps you have been baptized or have regularly attended church since you were a child. You may even serve and lead in your church. Baptism, worship attendance, and church involvement are all appropriate, obedient responses to a relationship with God. However, they don't create or replace the relationship. Was there an occasion in your life when you repented to God of your sins and asked Christ to be your Savior and Lord? If not, the most important thing you could possibly do is to obey what Scripture teaches and settle this matter with God here and now. Ask the Lord to speak to you as you read and think about the following Scriptures.

- □ Romans 3:23: All have sinned.
- □ Romans 6:23: Eternal life is a free gift of God.
- □ Romans 5:8: Because of His love, Jesus paid the death penalty for your sins.
- □ Romans 10:9-10: Confess Jesus as your Lord and acknowledge that God raised Him from the dead.
- □ Romans 10:13: Ask God to forgive your sins and trust Him to do so.

To place your faith in Jesus and receive His gift of eternal life, you must take the following steps.

- □ Recognize that God created you for a love relationship with Him. He wants you to love Him with all your being.
- □ Admit that you're a sinner and that you can't save yourself.
- □ Believe that Jesus paid the penalty for your sin by His death on the cross and that He rose from the dead in power and victory over death.
- □ Confess (agree with God about) your sins, which separate you from Him.
- □ Repent of (turn away from) your sins.
- □ Ask Jesus to save you by His grace, which is an undeserved gift of His love.
- □ Turn over the control of your life to Jesus.

If you need help, call on your group leader, a Christian friend, or a minister in your church. If you've just made this most important decision, tell your group the good news of what God has done in your life. Then share your decision with your church.

365-day devotional based on the modern classic *Experiencing God* by Henry Blackaby.

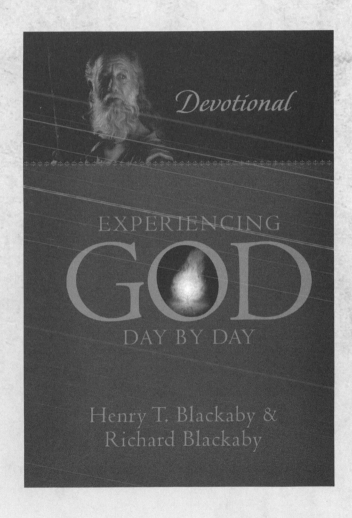